PATHOLOGICAL

The Murderous Rage of Dr. Anthony Garcia

HENRY J. CORDES
TODD COOPER

Omaha World-Herald

WILDBLUE
PRESS

WildBluePress.com

PATHOLOGICAL published by:

WILDBLUE PRESS
P.O. Box 102440
Denver, Colorado 80250

Publisher Disclaimer: Any opinions, statements of fact or fiction, descriptions, dialogue, and citations found in this book were provided by the author, and are solely those of the author. The publisher makes no claim as to their veracity or accuracy, and assumes no liability for the content.

Copyright 2018 by Omaha World-Herald

All rights reserved. No part of this book may be reproduced in any form or by any means without the prior written consent of the Publisher, excepting brief quotes used in reviews.

WILDBLUE PRESS is registered at the U.S. Patent and Trademark Offices.

ISBN 978-1-948239-01-1   Trade Paperback
ISBN 978-1-948239-00-4   eBook

Interior Formatting/Book Cover Design by Elijah Toten
www.totencreative.com

PATHOLOGICAL

The Murderous Rage of Dr. Anthony Garcia

TABLE OF CONTENTS

CHAPTER 1: 'WHAT THE HELL IS THIS?' 7

CHAPTER 2: TOM AND SHIRLEE 10

CHAPTER 3: THE MAN IN THE CRV 17

CHAPTER 4: IN HIS BLOOD 23

CHAPTER 5: SPINNING WHEELS 31

CHAPTER 6: COLD CASE 37

CHAPTER 7: MOTHER'S DAY 48

CHAPTER 8: CHANGE OF PLANS 53

CHAPTER 9: 'HE'S BACK' 59

CHAPTER 10: SERIAL KILLER AT LARGE 66

CHAPTER 11: THE TASK FORCE 70

CHAPTER 12: MORE THAN A NAME 75

CHAPTER 13: TEAM GARCIA 81

CHAPTER 14: THE TRIGGER 87

CHAPTER 15: THE BIG BREAK 101

CHAPTER 16: 'DO WE HAVE ENOUGH?' 105

CHAPTER 17: 'HE'S MOVING' 114

CHAPTER 18: THE RECKONING 120

CHAPTER 19: MISSED OPPORTUNITIES 123

CHAPTER 20: STRANGE WAYS 132

CHAPTER 21: THE NERD COP 150

CHAPTER 22: ONE FINAL PIECE 156

CHAPTER 23: COURTROOM COMBAT 160

CHAPTER 24: RYDER 167

CHAPTER 25: WITNESS ON TRIAL 171

CHAPTER 26: BREAKING POINT 177

CHAPTER 27: JUSTICE DONE 182

CHAPTER 28: EPILOGUE 189

PHOTOS 197

ACKNOWLEDGEMENTS 211

"And if you wrong us, shall we not revenge?"
—William Shakespeare, *The Merchant of Venice*

CHAPTER 1: 'WHAT THE HELL IS THIS?'

When police detective Derek Mois stepped over the threshold of the stately red brick home, he was immediately struck by the contrast between the everyday and the horrifying.

First to catch his eye were the cleaning supplies. A blue plastic bucket. A mop. A bright yellow bottle of Lysol. All casually set down in the middle of the entryway. And then just to the left, on the floor of an adjoining room, a waif of a boy with a knife through his neck.

It was the body of 11-year-old Tom Hunter, the gifted young son of the two doctors whose home Mois had just entered. Tom was splayed face-down on the blood-splattered dining room carpet. His spindly arms were straight as pins by his side, his bookish, wire-rimmed eyeglasses just above his head. Mois could see the knife's stainless steel handle protruding from the right side of the boy's neck, surrounded by an angry cluster of crimson stab wounds, both deep and superficial.

Mois' jaw tightened. A driven detective with short-cropped hair and sleeves of elaborate tattoos — still works in progress — going down both arms, the two-year veteran of Omaha's homicide unit had, unfortunately, seen dead kids before. And his experience confronting the handiwork of society's worst had long ago taught him to check his emotions as soon as he came through that front door.

But as a father with two young sons of his own, this sight was a punch in the gut, a memory that would never leave him. Who could do this? How cold, how callous, how depraved did someone have to be to stab a little boy until his life, future and promise drain away? This was about as ugly and evil as another human being could get.

Steeling himself, Mois walked through a set of French doors into a freshly cleaned kitchen. He right away spied on the immaculate counter a Farberware knife block, the knives' stainless steel handles matching what he'd just seen sticking from the boy's neck. Whoever killed the boy had drawn the murder weapon from right here in the kitchen.

Mois carefully stepped through the dinette, spotting Tom's shoes, backpack and hooded sweatshirt, all on the floor where he'd cast them off hours earlier. Mois heard an eerie sound coming from the basement stairwell, the theme music of the video game Tom had abandoned just before he died.

Following that sound, Mois turned the corner into a hallway and was confronted by a large pool of blood and the second body he'd been told about. This was Shirlee Sherman, the Hunter family's 57-year-old house cleaner. Mois could see Shirlee likewise had a steel kitchen knife protruding from her neck — clearly the killer's calling card.

The blue paisley scarf Sherman had donned for her cleaning that day still covered her head. As with Tom, she'd suffered numerous stab wounds, all concentrated along the right side of her neck.

Mois could already see this grim scene was an extreme departure from the gang- or drug-related shootings that were the staple of homicide work in Omaha, both the victims and perpetrators usually no strangers to law enforcement. Almost everything about these murders was different.

A grandmother and a young boy as victims.

Killed with knives left impaled in their necks.

In a gorgeous home filled with valuables — all completely undisturbed.

And perhaps most troubling, no obvious suspect or motive.

Later as Mois worked into the gray hours just before dawn documenting the crime scene, he held an aside with his sergeant, speaking just out of the earshot of the crime lab technicians working nearby.

"Holy shit," Mois told his supervisor. "What the hell is this?"

It was a question Mois would spend more than five years trying to answer.

CHAPTER 2: TOM AND SHIRLEE

It was a brilliant March 13, the radiant sunshine and balmy air a reminder that while winter on the Great Plains wasn't officially over yet, it was losing its icy grip.

A school bus lurched to a halt in front of a home on North 54th Street in Dundee, one of the most desirable streets in one of Omaha's most distinctive old neighborhoods. Tom Hunter popped up like a gopher from his seat in the very back, glided down the aisle and bounded down to the street. Dressed for the mild weather in a lightweight, striped blue hoodie, Tom walked past the last surviving patch of snow melting in the sloped front yard and entered his house around the back.

Elsewhere around Dundee, an affluent neighborhood known throughout Omaha for its old-fashioned globe-style street lights, life on this Thursday in 2008 was moving to a familiar mid-afternoon rhythm.

Dana Boyle watched Tom's 3:18 p.m. return through her living room window across the street. Five months pregnant and feeling every bit of it, she was grabbing some much-needed rest on the couch. Not for long, though, she now knew. For the sight and sound of Tom's bus served as a daily touchstone for the full-time mom, a reminder it was almost time to meet her own 7-year-old son after school.

Just down the street, Katie Swanson also prepared for her kids' imminent return from school. Deciding this would be a great day to shake off winter, she pulled out of storage her "Slow Children at Play" signs. She later placed the unofficial traffic signs down at "the Pie," a wedge-shaped, grassy median where 54th Street kids had gathered to play for generations.

This was Omaha circa 2008, a thriving Midwest metropolis of some 850,000 people that was little like anything imagined by those who saw the state of Nebraska as rural flyover country. The former cow town actually boasted the headquarters of five Fortune 500 companies — for its size, more than New York, Los Angeles or Chicago. It was probably best known, though, as home to famed investment wizard Warren Buffett, one of the wealthiest men on the planet. The Oracle of Omaha, in fact, lived in a relatively modest Dundee home just blocks from where Tom Hunter hopped off his bus.

Not far removed from his own pre-adolescent play dates at the Pie, this street and this spacious home were the only ones Tom had known in his life. Now just three months shy of his 12th birthday, Tom had grown into a bright and worldly kid who seemed destined for big things.

Tom was the youngest of four children — all boys — of Drs. William and Claire Hunter. Both parents worked as practicing and teaching physicians at Omaha's Creighton University School of Medicine. Befitting his parents' professional status, Tom enjoyed a privileged, idyllic childhood on 54th Street. Eight years younger than his next closest brother, Tom had always been a delightfully precocious child. He interacted easily with those much older, possessed a mischievous grin and always had something to say.

At nearby Dundee Elementary, Tom proved an academic prodigy, something that for his parents came to be both a blessing and curse. Tending to pick things up quickly, Tom found homework rote and boring. He put it off. He rebelled.

Why should I have to do all this stuff when I already know it? The Hunters had to hound him daily, his father often sitting down with him in the living room to force him to fill out his math tables or diagram his sentences for English.

Such battles waned when Tom left local Dundee Elementary School after fourth grade and transferred to King Science and Technology Center. In that inner-city magnet school, Tom found a true home for his intellectual gifts. At King, Tom was able to indulge his fascination for all things scientific and technical. The school even had its own planetarium. Tom seemed poised to shoot for the stars himself. His teachers could easily see the well-liked kid who smiled through silver braces following his parents into medicine or some branch of the sciences.

Outside of school, Tom loved to read, getting his hands on the latest Harry Potter tome as soon as it hit the bookstore shelf and devouring it in hours. Tom even looked a bit like the young wizard Harry, with his roundish eyeglasses and mop of brown hair.

Books aside, Tom really wanted to play football, a sport his slight build — not to mention his parents — wouldn't allow him to play. Instead, he competed for years in the local YMCA basketball league. A regular ritual for father and son was a Saturday morning game at the Y followed by lunch at one of Tom's favorite fast-food restaurants. The boy enjoyed close relationships with both of his parents.

Tom also had lots of neighborhood friends, and they tended to travel in a pack. They'd play basketball in the school yard or go buy candy in Dundee's quaint old business district. He and his friends would also often beat paths to each other's homes to play video games. Favorites included various violent shoot-'em-ups and Madden football, where Tom competed as his beloved Green Bay Packers. As Tom roamed the quiet and safe streets of his neighborhood, his parents' rule was simple: Be home by 6 for dinner.

Treasured family snapshots from the time captured Tom just being Tom: intently at the controls of a video game; relishing a stimulating visit to the Smithsonian in Washington; suited up for basketball; at rest on the same couch where his dad once forced him do his math; patting the family cat outside on a brilliant day — a day much like this March day.

Now near the end of sixth grade, Tom was a latch-key kid, his parents trusting him to take care of himself in the two to three hours before they got home from Creighton. He entered the house just like the careless pre-teen he was, kicking off his black Adidas shoes and dumping his hoodie and backpack right on the floor.

This being Thursday, Tom also knew it was the one day each week he didn't arrive to a completely empty house. Thursday was cleaning day in the Hunter home, the day Shirlee Sherman came to scrub, dust and vacuum.

The 57-year-old Sherman was a resilient, no-nonsense woman who had endured some tough times — many of them traced to her unwavering willingness to put the happiness of others ahead of her own. As one of her brothers would later put it, "She got a raw deal in a lot of things in life."

The former Shirlee Waite grew up in a working-class neighborhood of Omaha with three siblings and four close cousins — all of them boys. So, during her early years, Shirlee turned her back on dolls in favor of baseball, basketball and box hockey, often besting the Waite boys in those pursuits. As the oldest, Shirlee stood up for her kin on the playground and helped care for them at home, a role that particularly grew after her parents divorced. She never argued or complained. She just did it. It was the beginning of a lifetime of Shirlee shouldering the burdens of family.

Her brothers considered Shirlee the smart one. But by the time she got to Omaha's Central High School, she didn't have much use for books. She followed a fairly traditional track at the time for a girl from a blue-collar family. Within six months of getting her diploma in 1968, she was married, and in short order she gave birth to a daughter.

Shirlee worked tending bar and at one point ran a tavern that her father owned. But that didn't last long. After her parents' divorce, the stubborn, opinionated Shirlee didn't always see eye to eye with her dad. Sherman's own marriage fell apart shortly after her second child, a son, was born in 1974. That's when she largely turned to cleaning houses. It gave the single mom the flexibility to work around her kids' schedules. And with her strong work ethic and barkeep's friendly demeanor, Sherman had no trouble landing jobs.

Many of her clients came to have ties to Creighton's medical school, her name passed around among doctors there. Sherman had come highly recommended to the Hunters and had now cleaned their home for almost two years.

By this point, Shirlee's children had grown and long since left the house. She had bad knees, a smoker's wheeze and lines in her face carved by the tough times. She'd reached a point in life when she should have been able to give more time to herself. But true to her nature, she remained the Waite family caretaker and glue, her days still revolving around the wellbeing of others.

She talked to her elderly mother every day and visited a few times a week. Often she would bring fresh-cut flowers or vegetables from the big garden she tended every summer. In fact, anyone visiting the generous Shirlee would inevitably leave with a bag of whatever was in season.

One of her greatest joys in life was spending time with her five grandchildren. Shirlee had a huge capacity for kids. Any extra money she saved would inevitably go to make sure they had what they needed.

Daughter Kelly, herself now a single mom, lived in the house right next door to Shirlee. That certainly had its benefits. Shirlee cherished her time with 6-year-old granddaughter Madison. Shirlee would often see Madison in the morning and then care for her after school until her mom got home.

But that living arrangement had also recently been a source of tension and conflict between Shirlee and her daughter. Shirlee had big problems with the latest man in Kelly's life. For one, he was married. Most alarming to Shirlee, though, was his violent temper. Several times he'd lashed out in her daughter's home, kicking in the front door or punching a hole in the wall. Shirlee had warned Kelly, "It's going to be you next."

It was of course no surprise to Shirlee when in March 2007, the boyfriend broke Kelly's jaw in three places. Police arrested him for felony assault. But like so many women caught up in abusive relationships, Kelly refused to swear off the creep. Even after he broke her jaw, she'd try to sneak around to see him behind Shirlee's back. It drove Shirlee bat crazy. She knew men like this from her bartender days. He wouldn't change. So she vowed to do everything possible to keep them apart.

Since Shirlee held the deed to Kelly's house, she tried to legally keep the boyfriend away. She called the cops on him for property damage. She had his car towed. Though of medium build, Shirlee proved fearless as a wildcat in confronting the boyfriend. "She would literally get right in his face," Shirlee's brother, Brad Waite, would recall years later. " 'Go ahead and hit me.' "

Shirlee also told the Hunters of the abusive boyfriend, the subject coming up after she failed to show up to clean one day. "I'm going to get the SOB if it's the last thing I do," she said. The nurturing Shirlee was concerned for more than just Kelly's safety. Shirlee didn't want Madison exposed to the violence. "I need to protect my granddaughter," she'd written in a court affidavit.

As Shirlee cleaned that day in March 2008, those concerns for Madison had not diminished. In fact, it's very likely Shirlee had thoughts of Madison as she room-by-room worked her way through the Hunter house. She was due to pick her grandchild up from daycare as soon as she was done.

It's unknown whether Sherman greeted the young Tom Hunter when he came home from school that day — they typically tried to stay out of each other's way — but it seems possible she did. Because at some point, Tom went upstairs where Shirlee was cleaning to change into a favorite pair of long black basketball shorts. He left piles of clothes all over the floor as he dug the shorts from the bottom of the drawer.

Tom's parents would have preferred he at that point launch right into his homework. But as was often the case, Tom figured homework could wait. He popped open a can of Dr. Pepper, foraged a bag of SunChips from the pantry and headed to the basement to play his Xbox 360.

That's how he would spend the final carefree minutes of his life.

CHAPTER 3: THE MAN IN THE CRV

Boyle, the Hunters' across-the-street neighbor, was the first to notice the silver Honda CRV as it moved conspicuously up her street.

She had just left the house around 3:20 p.m. to meet her son after school. Right in front of her, she saw the CRV herky-jerky starting and stopping as it went north up 54th, as if the driver was scouting for an address. When the vehicle paused in front of the Hunter home, the driver, a dark-haired man with olive skin, peered back at Boyle through his rear-view mirror. Just for a moment, their eyes met.

It seemed to Boyle the man was spooked by that. Because he quickly started back up and followed the curve of the street to the right and out of sight. Boyle thought the driver's behavior a little odd. She noted the car had some kind of unfamiliar out-of-state plate — white with pastel colors like pink or peach. But Boyle's first thoughts of the man were benign. He must be checking out a home that's soon coming on the market, she thought. This was the kind of street where houses often sold by word of mouth before a for-sale sign ever showed up in the yard.

Other neighbors saw the same man after he drove the silver CRV around the corner and parked a couple blocks south down 53rd Street. The driver just sat there for a minute or so. Then he emerged into the broad daylight and started walking back up the street. The man was wearing a dark, oversized jacket over a white collared shirt and dark pants. He also had a dark canvas messenger bag slung over his shoulder, as if on some kind of business. As would become apparent, he definitely was.

Most who saw him that day recognized him as an outsider. For one neighbor, the giveaway was his ill-fitting suit, not like the tailored ones her husband wore. The darker tone of his skin also made him stand out in the nearly all-white neighborhood, the man later described to police variously as Hispanic or of Middle Eastern descent.

Mary Rommelfanger was alerted to the stranger's arrival in front of her house by her dog's barks. The dutiful Charlie never failed to alert the family to ominous threats like a UPS package delivery or kids zipping by on skateboards. But Rommelfanger did become suspicious after watching the way this man lingered in his car. After he finally exited the vehicle, she even went upstairs to a second-story window just so she could track him as he walked north up 53rd. Soon, he disappeared from sight.

Minutes later, when Rommelfanger left to pick up her daughter from school, she noted in her rear-view mirror that the CRV had no front license plate. She vowed to write down the number of the back plate when she returned. But she never did get that chance. Because by the time she and her daughter came home an hour later after an unscheduled stop for Slurpees prompted by the nice weather, the car was already gone.

Paul Medin became the next neighbor to size up the stranger. Medin was walking to pick up his son from Dundee Elementary around 3:30 p.m. when he saw the man walk around the corner in front of him and turn on to 54th Street. The man stumbled — Medin thought it must have been a sidewalk crack, but there would be speculation years later that the man had been drinking. Then the stranger proceeded to the front door of the Hunter home.

From the Hunters' front porch, the man looked back directly at Medin a couple of times, sending off a creepy vibe. "I can't explain this," Medin would say years later. "But I had a bad feeling about what was happening." Medin even made a point of noting the address number of this unfamiliar house, just in case he heard of something suspicious going on.

The man must have knocked or rung, because after a while he appeared to be talking to someone through the storm door. It seemed to Medin the person who answered the door was a woman, but police would later speculate it was more likely the mop-haired Tom. As Medin walked on, he couldn't help taking one last look back. The man was gone. Medin could only assume he'd been let inside.

Some 10 minutes would pass. That's when Swanson then saw the man leave the Hunter house and walk toward her as she supervised her kids' play at the Pie. To her, the man was walking casually, not seeming in any hurry, not betraying the least bit of concern.

As a protective mom — there was a reason she was out there with her traffic-calming, children-at-play signs — Swanson felt a bit uneasy seeing this stranger walk toward her kids. "He didn't look like he belonged," she'd later say. So she was relieved when he made a quick turn east on Davenport, back in the direction of his parked car, and strolled out of sight. Soon after, the CRV was gone, too.

It would be hours before Swanson or anyone else learned of the wicked nature of this mystery man's call in Dundee.

* * *

For Dr. William "Bill" Hunter, the first sign something was amiss was Shirlee's car. As Hunter turned up his driveway around 5:45 p.m., he was surprised to see his house cleaner's white Ford Taurus still parked by the back door. Shirlee must be running behind, he thought — not unheard of if she got a late start on her cleaning.

After his long day at the office, Hunter was looking forward to spending the evening at home with Tom. Since wife Claire had flown off to a medical training conference in Hawaii, it would be up to Bill to throw dinner together and make sure Tom was ready for another school day.

Hunter walked through the back door, set down his briefcase and reached his jacket toward the white coat rack in the corner. That's when, with a start, he spotted Sherman.

She was face down on the hardwood floor of the hallway. He saw the knife through her neck. Even in this surreal moment, he recognized it immediately as coming from the knife block in the kitchen. Hunter could also tell from the sheer volume of blood surrounding Shirlee that she was dead.

As a practicing and teaching doctor of pathology — the medical specialty devoted to disease and how it impacts the human body — seeing a corpse was actually an everyday event for Hunter. At Creighton's teaching hospital, the pathologist regularly supervised doctors-in-training who were conducting autopsies. To Hunter, death was natural, clinical and most often easily explained.

But to now see the body of someone he knew sprawled in a bloody pool on the floor of his own home jarred Hunter to his core. And just as suddenly, a panicked thought sent his heart racing: Tom. Where's Tom?

Hunter could hear the soundtrack of his son's Xbox game repeating on a loop in the basement, a sound he would describe years later as "that horrible music." And the stairs that led down to the basement were just to the left of Sherman's body. Hunter darted halfway down and quickly scanned the room. No Tom.

Racing back up, his breath getting shorter with each step, he anxiously called out his son's name. "Tom! Tom!" Hunter went through a sitting room in the rear of the home, again seeing nothing, and then into the living room. It was from there, looking across the front entryway into the adjoining formal dining room, that Hunter first laid eyes on his son.

Tom was face down on the floor. He, too, had a knife sticking all the way through his neck. Hunter could also tell by all the blood soaking the elegant blue rug that his son was dead. Just to be sure, the doctor checked Tom's cold wrist for a pulse.

Hunter struggled to get his mind around what he was seeing. Is this real? He stepped around his son's body and staggered over to the phone in the kitchen. He knew he needed help, but he couldn't think who to call. He took a few deep breaths before dialing 9-1-1. And even then, the flabbergasted father struggled with what to say.

"Do you need a rescue squad?" the emergency operator asked.

"No, these two are deceased," he replied, slipping into the clinical language of his work. "I need the police."

The operator told Hunter to leave the house immediately and sit on the front porch to await help. Hunter complied but couldn't sit, quietly pacing back and forth. He was still unable to grasp the horror of what he'd just seen. Indeed, Hunter would long be haunted by the unimaginable images in his home that day. He would soon after undergo treatment for Post Traumatic Stress Disorder. It would take a year of therapy for him to cope with the nightmarish scene he'd witnessed.

Those traumatic struggles would only be layered on top of the profound grief over losing Tom. To have his son so viciously stolen from his family was a heartbreak that would never, ever, go away.

The neighborhood was soon swarming with Omaha cops and cruisers. They sealed off the Hunters' street. They fanned out in the neighborhood, hearing for the first time about the mystery man who had so casually come and gone hours earlier.

Rommelfanger gasped when she learned that one of her son's best friends had been murdered right around the corner from her own home. She also knew immediately that the man she'd watched park out front hours earlier had been the culprit. "Oh my God," she exclaimed. "I saw him!"

To have a neighborhood kid and grandmother so brutally slain sent immediate shock waves through Dundee that reverberated all over Omaha. If this could happen in one of the city's quietest, most affluent neighborhoods, was anyone truly safe?

Omaha police officials attempted to tamp down the fear. A department spokesman the next morning offered few details on the nature of the deaths but said the killings appeared to be "an isolated incident."

But the truth was, at that moment, the Omaha police had no idea of the killer's identity.

CHAPTER 4: IN HIS BLOOD

As detective Derek Mois worked with crime lab technicians that first night noting, marking, photographing and collecting any relevant evidence, the detective was already crafting his theories of what had happened in the Hunter home. He looked hard at the bodies, their positioning, the injuries. What were these voiceless victims telling him?

Mois attempted to put himself in the footsteps of a killer.

Tom almost certainly was killed first, Mois surmised. He had probably left his video game to respond to the man at the door. The killer then either talked or forced his way in, or maybe snuck in around the back after being rebuffed. When Shirlee was cleaning, Mois learned, the back door would typically be unlocked.

The theory that Tom died first was supported by the fact that Mois found a substance around Tom's mouth that had subsequently been smeared on the back of Shirlee's bright blue blouse — what's known in detective parlance as a "fluid transfer."

Shirlee was most likely cleaning upstairs when Tom was attacked. Mois found her vacuum still plugged into the wall in the master bedroom and her scrub brush in the bathtub. Shirlee may have come downstairs to drop off the cleaning supplies in the hall, or perhaps had come at the curious sound of Tom's struggle. And then she found herself face-to-face with a vicious killer.

It made complete sense that she would then attempt to flee down the hallway toward the back door. From her body position and injuries, Mois believed she'd been chased down from behind, pushed to the floor and then dispatched after a brief struggle.

Mois was in his element as he pieced together the violent sequence of events. In his relatively brief stint in Omaha's homicide unit, he'd already proven himself adept at reconstructing crimes, using his keen eye for detail and logical sense to pull it all together.

A 34-year-old Minnesota native, Mois had moved to Omaha and joined its police force nine years earlier. He'd previously worked as a police officer in Washington state, in a mountain town so small he could sometimes work a 12-hour shift and not get a single call. Mois craved more action. But it wasn't a macho thing with him. He truly felt a need to be part of something bigger, a chance to serve and make a difference in the world.

Mois looked for police jobs all over the country before a friend recommended he apply in Omaha, a job that would ultimately bring him back to his Midwestern roots. His rookie photo coming out of the academy showed a fresh-faced cop with short dark hair, a sturdy jaw and piercing blue eyes. He looked like a man with big intentions.

After more than four years as a street cop, Mois gravitated toward detective work. For two years he investigated car thieves, burglars and other sticky-fingered types. It was a little aggravating. Caseloads were high, with limited ability to focus on any one. And even when he'd make good busts, the perps usually did short stints in prison and then were right back in business. They were never going to change. That life was all they knew. "You do what you can," he'd say of those years. "But it's frustrating."

Still, Mois' work soon caught the eye of the lieutenant who ran Omaha's homicide squad. There had been a brutal theft case, a violent purse snatching in which the elderly victim suffered a broken hip and later died. Mois was able to find the offender and then pinned so many other crimes on him that he was locked up for a good long time. After that, the homicide lieutenant, Alex Hayes, started recruiting Mois to join his unit.

Mois at first resisted. He knew homicide detectives in Omaha worked ungodly hours. He'd be on call 24/7. And as the new grunt of the unit, Mois knew he'd be called in on every weekend and late-night shooting — common events when summer arrived and the gang turf wars heated up. Since Mois was newly married and he and his wife were just starting a family, he turned Hayes down at least twice.

But Hayes persisted. And in 2005 when the lieutenant had another opening, he sat Mois down. In homicide, you will be tested like nowhere else, Hayes told him. Everything you do is scrutinized to the Nth degree. The defense attorneys turn any misstep into an opening to get a killer off. It's not a place for sloppy, half-assed police work. Challenge yourself. This is where you belong.

"In that conversation, I wanted it all the sudden," Mois would say years later. He signed on.

Hayes and other veterans mentored Mois, schooling him on the myriad ways and means by which human beings kill each other. Hayes would often assign senior detectives to put Mois in their pocket for the day, show the rookie the ropes. Hayes would also test Mois and ask his opinion on cases, bluntly pointing out where Mois was wrong. The boss more than once told Mois his answer was "the stupidest fucking thing I ever heard." But Mois appreciated Hayes' direct approach and leadership. He looked up to him.

Mois found that the reality of being a homicide detective was every bit as challenging as he'd thought. His life became a never-ending cycle of drive-by shootings and other violent mayhem. He was racking up more than 600 hours of overtime a year, demands that were not real popular at home.

But he took great satisfaction in putting away some of the most dangerous people in society, at times starting from nothing. He even liked taking the stand in court, a part of the job many colleagues loathed. Mois also loved the camaraderie in his unit, guys doing their best to keep things loose as they went about their serious, macabre work. It's an attitude that would later be summed up by words emblazoned on the coffee mug of a colleague: "Homicide: Our day begins where yours ends." At the same time, Mois continued to impress fellow detectives with his dedication and professionalism.

Around Omaha's detective bureau, the free-spirited Mois in many ways marched to his own drum. He was an atheist attracted to Buddhist philosophy who was mostly surrounded by conservative Christians. His simple, guiding philosophy to life was to judge others only by their actions and leave the world a better place.

Mois also wasn't keen on the department's dress code. He'd string a tie around his neck only when a supervisor threatened to write him up. He had a collection of assorted ties and sport coats hanging on the wall above his desk, mostly gathering dust. He came to work most days in comfortable, non-regulation hiking boots. And the elaborate Buddhist- and Norse-themed tattoos that over time came to cover both of his muscular arms sometimes showed below his rolled-up shirtsleeves.

But when it came to solving Omaha's most violent crimes, Mois' work was always by the book, meticulous and intensely thorough. Just three months earlier at Christmastime, a troubled teen walked into an Omaha department store with a high-powered assault rifle and senselessly snuffed out eight innocent souls before turning the gun on himself. It was the deadliest mall shooting in U.S. history, adding Omaha to the long, sobering list of American cities jarred by mass shootings.

In the aftermath, the methodical Mois — by then a two-year veteran of homicide — was hand-picked by his superiors to document the crime scene on the store's third floor, where seven of the nine bodies lay. His peers knew he would do things by the numbers and get everything right.

Mois also stood out for the way he passionately poured himself into his cases — a drive that was motivated, he'd say, by his empathy for the families shattered by murder.

Investigating homicides often meant spending much time with the families of the victims as he tried to discern who had motive to kill them. Mois would almost inevitably form a bond with those grieving families, coming to take their losses personally.

"They want answers, and the only people they can turn to is us," he'd later say. "You can't do what we do and not get affected by the families. It's just not possible." Mois would always keep a snowflake Christmas ornament on his desk, a meaningful keepsake given to him by one of the families devastated by the department store massacre.

Not only did Mois feel a personal obligation to solve his cases, but the cool, self-possessed cop was also confident that he could. As he now worked the bloody scene in the Hunter home, Mois wanted nothing more than to be able to say to the Hunter and Waite families that the person who stole away Tom and Shirlee was now in jail.

While Mois' affinity for crime scenes was one reason he worked the Hunter house now, the assignment was mostly a matter of happenstance. The bodies had been found a couple hours after Mois began his 3 p.m. evening shift that day. As this complex, baffling case would unfold in months and years to come, this would be just the first of several remarkable instances where Mois just happened to be the man in the right place.

As Mois looked around the Hunter home, he saw valuables in every room. Computers. A brand new digital camera and big lens. Entertainment equipment. Nice furnishings. Nice everything. None of it touched. Sherman's purse, holding $800 she'd just collected as rent on a property she owned, still sat on the dinette table where she always left it. The only room that looked ransacked was Tom's bedroom, but Mois later learned from Bill Hunter it was just a case of Tom being Tom. To Mois, this was clearly no robbery or burglary. So why were Tom and Shirlee killed?

The knives were also a curious thing. In addition to the blades left in the victims' necks, two other knives had been pulled from the block. Mois found one beneath Tom and another sitting atop a stack of *Bon Appetit* cooking magazines on the dining table.

Why were the victims killed with knives taken right from the home? If the man in the suit had come with intent to kill, wouldn't he have brought his own weapon? Had he killed in spur-of-the-moment rage? Was he familiar with this house?

It was also curious that the culprit seemed to come and go so brazenly, in broad daylight. Why was this guy so unconcerned by all the neighbors who saw him? That, and the pastel-colored, unfamiliar license plate, made Mois surmise the killer may not have been from Omaha.

The stab wounds seemed the most significant part of this mystery. Mois had seen more than his share of stabbing deaths. When someone pulls a knife, it's typically a wild, angry event, the victim stabbed and slashed all over. Here, it seemed the wounds were delivered with purpose, confined on both victims to the same small area on the right side of the neck. "The wounds kind of baffled us," he'd say later. "They were so extreme."

But Mois would soon have more light shed on the nature of the wounds to Tom and Shirlee. Because after Mois stayed up all night processing the Hunter crime scene, he headed straight for the county morgue to witness the autopsies. Mois looked on as Dr. Jerry Jones, the pathologist on duty that day, removed the knives — a 5-inch blade from Tom, a 7-inch blade from Shirlee. Then Jones documented the products of the killer's cruel work, numbering all the wounds.

With both victims, some of the cuts were superficial, as if the killer was probing with the blade or inflicting torture. Others were clearly deep and gaping. Shirlee had suffered 18 distinct cutting wounds around her neck. On both victims, most all the wounds were clustered below the right ear and jaw line. "Is there a reason he would stab them there?" Mois asked Jones.

Sure, Jones replied. The wounds appeared to target the carotid artery and jugular vein, both critical for blood flow to the head. Severing those lifelines would very quickly incapacitate and kill the victims. And indeed, Jones would ultimately find in his internal probing that in both victims, both the carotid and jugular had been completely severed. If the killer truly was "going for the jugular," he seemed to know what he was doing. An ominous thought popped into Mois' head: Maybe he has done this before.

By the time Mois wrapped up at the morgue and turned for home, he'd been working close to 30 hours. His wife and two young sons were already asleep.

But even after all he'd been through, Mois wasn't ready to rest. He couldn't if he tried.

So instead, he went out the back door to the wood deck he'd years earlier built by hand. It was time for an emotional reset.

With big oak and ash trees towering overhead, the deck always served as the detective's sanctuary after a bad day at the office. A day where he had to notify a family of a loved one's death. Or a day, like this one, where he'd witnessed unspeakable carnage.

Other than the department store massacre — where there was so much blood a metallic, iron scent permeated the air, so thick Mois could taste it — no crime scene would ever weigh on him more than the one he witnessed in the Hunter home. But like the many other type-A toughs who seem to gravitate to police work, for Mois these were things you simply didn't talk to others about. He internalized all his feelings from the day.

In the darkness, Mois pulled up a chair, put his feet up on the railing and listened to the peaceful solitude of his suburban neighborhood. He did his best to decompress, disengage and turn the feelings off. Still, the father in Mois made it hard for him to avoid thoughts of young Tom.

More than once in the past 24 hours, Mois had to take a deep breath and emotionally re-collect himself as he thought about Tom's ghastly final moments. The detective pictured it in his mind: the terror the 11-year-old boy must have endured. And in the place where he should have felt safest — at home, waiting for his dad.

Out on his deck that night, Mois knew this, too: The monster capable of such evil still lurked out there, free to lash out again.

CHAPTER 5: SPINNING WHEELS

Bill Hunter was in shock and not thinking completely straight when he sat down for his first interview with Omaha detectives, about an hour after finding his son with a knife through his neck. During an emotionally grueling session at Omaha police headquarters downtown, his interrogators gently pressed him, at times asking uncomfortable questions.

Any marital problems between you and Claire?

Are you having any problems with neighbors?

Do you have any patients upset with you? Does your wife?

Are you having any trouble with gambling?

Do you have any suspicion of the boys using drugs?

Do you have any idea who or why somebody would do this?

In obvious anguish and frustration, Hunter covered his face with both hands. At other times, he rested his forehead flat on the table and groaned. Hunter simply had no answers. He just could not imagine who could have done something so ruthless and horrific to his family. "Honestly, I'm racking my brain," he told the two detectives, desperation in his voice. "We live a peaceful existence, almost ridiculously simple."

Indeed, there were scores of questions and few answers as Omaha detectives collectively sought to learn what happened inside the Hunter house on March 13, 2008. Seven detectives were initially assigned to work the case that around the department came to be known simply by the name of the quiet neighborhood where the crime occurred: "Dundee."

It was obvious to everyone that the key to solving Dundee would be found in identifying the olive-skinned man driving the silver CRV. It seemed clear he had come with intent to kill, the reason he had parked around the corner from the Hunter house. This seemed premeditated murder. But who was he? Where did he come from?

Whoever he was, he'd been able to slip in and out of the Hunter house like a ghost, leaving no physical trace. The crime lab found no relevant DNA or fingerprints anywhere in the house. Essentially the only solid lead they had on him was the CRV. But with no plate number, there were literally thousands of vehicles on the road that fit that description.

To aid in the suspect's identification, an artist within days rendered neighbors' collected observations into a composite sketch, depicting the profile of a man with dark eyes and dark, close-cropped hair. And as Mois would later put it, the drawing generated "a shit ton of tips" after it was released to the media.

The vast majority of the tips coming in were from callers suggesting the drawing looked vaguely like someone they knew: the guy who fixed their car, or a man who used to live down the street. Detectives would run down nearly all such tips, almost always finding the person mentioned had zero connection to either of the two victims. Eventually, Omaha police asked the media to stop running the image. All it seemed to produce was dozens of false leads.

To spur other tips, a reward fund was quickly established, one that would, ultimately, with the help of Sherman's family, grow to more than $50,000. Its size spoke to how much these slayings had traumatized the city. In all, Omaha police would log some 148 various tips during the first two months of the investigation, sending detectives looking in dozens of different directions.

"What everybody's asking is, 'Who could have done this, and why?'" said Dr. Roger Brumback, Hunter's boss and the chair of the Creighton University pathology department.

As Omaha detectives set out to answer that question, they faced a major barrier: No one even knew who the killer was targeting. Could Shirlee have been the intended victim? Was it Tom? Perhaps Drs. Bill or Claire Hunter, or even one of their older sons, was the true target. There was no obvious place to start.

Detectives turned to "victimology," diving deep into the backgrounds of all of those people to see if anyone they'd been in contact with could have had motive to kill.

Right away, detectives learned about Shirlee's battles with her daughter and her daughter's violent boyfriend. There was also evidence of past drug use within Shirlee's family. Perhaps the killings had been in retaliation for some kind of drug deal gone bad.

Shirlee's brothers at first were very suspicious of the violent boyfriend. As one of them would later put it, they gave him to police "on a platter." And Omaha detectives indeed were hot for him, too, putting him on the front burner of the investigation. They questioned him at length and did so on numerous occasions, once picking him up in the middle of the night to drag him downtown. They even tailed him.

But in the end, they also cleared him. His alibi for the time of the killings appeared solid. And the detectives also decided there was no reason to think he even knew Shirlee was at the Hunter home that day. The Waite family also eventually decided the boyfriend couldn't have done it. Police told them the assailant had gotten out of the Hunter house so cleanly, it was almost like a professional hit. The Waite family decided this guy couldn't have pulled off something like that.

As part of the victimology work, both Bill and Claire Hunter were questioned numerous times in the early days. Claire Hunter had learned of her son's death in a phone call while in Hawaii. A dear friend who saw the sketchy early news reports on TV told her "something awful" had happened in her home. For all Claire knew at the time, the two unnamed victims being referred to were her husband and Tom, fears that were only fueled when Bill failed to answer her frantic phone calls. She didn't know that at the moment, he was downtown being questioned.

When a detective in the interrogation room finally answered Bill's phone, Claire was adamant: You let me talk to my husband. Now. Bill got on and calmly broke the heartbreaking news. "I don't know what happened," he told her.

After her long, empty flight back to Omaha, Claire proved an emotional rock, helping her family pick up the pieces and arrange for the burial of her youngest child. But only a mother could truly appreciate the pain, grief and pangs of loss that stirred within Claire's strong exterior.

Detectives wanted both Hunters to think of anyone from their past who could have been driven to do this. During decades-long tenures at Creighton's medical center, both had come into contact with countless co-workers, students and patients.

Bill Hunter, a San Francisco native, had taught at Creighton since 1980. And since 2000, in addition to teaching duties, he had headed the school's residency program in pathology. In that role, he oversaw the new medical school graduates — known in the business as residents — who came to Creighton to receive training in pathology as their chosen medical specialty.

Claire, a Kansas City native, similarly oversaw young doctors seeking advanced training in cardiology. While Bill as a pathologist did not tend to interact with many patients or their families — instead consulting or performing tests related to patients under the care of other doctors — Claire had provided direct care for thousands of heart patients. Certainly a few of them over the years had some gripes.

During one early joint interview with the Hunters at their home, detectives did their best to prompt the doctors. They even suggested they draw up a list of people with possible grudges. It proved a short list. Bill Hunter would recall it included a disgruntled doctor-trainee Claire Hunter had worked with; and two medical students Bill Hunter had recently given bad reviews, including one who made what could be interpreted as a vague threat against another Creighton staffer on Facebook.

Bill Hunter offered little encouragement to police that they'd find any Creighton connection to these deaths. While he could think of other students he dealt with who had conflicts with the pathology department or Creighton, he didn't see where their issues were with him personally. In the end, he simply found it hard to believe anyone he'd been associated with at Creighton could have committed these horrible crimes.

The Hunters were also grilled about neighbors, home repair contractors and delivery drivers. Police ultimately dug into the Hunters' phone records, email accounts and finances, just to be sure there wasn't anything they were hiding. Investigators talked to others at Creighton, including nurses and staff who worked with the Hunters. No one was beyond scrutiny.

Mois also talked to the Hunters as part of the initial assignment he was given in Dundee: determining if young Tom had been the primary target. Mois would spend weeks learning about the boy's teachers, bus drivers, basketball coaches and camp counselors. Did any of them appear to have a special or inappropriate interest in the boy?

There was no evidence Tom had been assaulted sexually in the attack. Still, Mois had to consider the potential that this was the work of some kind of sexual predator. But after weeks of interviews and scoping the backgrounds of dozens of people, Mois found nothing that appeared out of line.

Investigators were also interested in possible ties between the Dundee killings and the murder the previous year of another Omaha woman. Intriguingly, that victim, Joy Blanchard, had also been stabbed in the neck with a knife taken right from her home. And as in Dundee, the knife was left impaled in her neck. That was hardly something you saw every day. In fact, longtime detectives in homicide could not recall any other cases where that happened.

Though detectives didn't have enough evidence to make an arrest in Blanchard's death, they had a pretty good idea one of her relatives had killed her. They looked hard for possible ties between that male relative and any of the victims in Dundee. In the end, that also went nowhere. Another theory discounted. Another road to nowhere.

Days turned to weeks, weeks turned to months. Most of the best leads and most promising lines of inquiry were being exhausted one by one. Even the detectives working the case could see it: The Dundee investigation was faltering. They also knew that time was now the enemy. With each passing day, it became less and less likely this murder mystery would ever be solved.

CHAPTER 6: COLD CASE

Most of the detectives originally assigned to Dundee slowly drifted off over the summer to pursue more recent murders. The killing never stops. There was a shooting involving white gang members from a suburban high school, a crime that proved violent gang activity wasn't limited to the inner city. And a couple of cases where parents were gunned down right in front of their terrified toddler children.

Those crimes needed to be investigated, too. While the Omaha police department had committed considerable resources to Dundee, they weren't unlimited. Still, department brass didn't want the investigation of such a high-profile case to die. So late that summer, they tabbed 42-year-old Scott Warner to take the lead.

Warner was an Air Force veteran who had spent 16 years as an Omaha cop, including time in a cruiser, on bike patrol and even astride a horse as part of the department's mounted patrol. He'd been an investigator for several years now. And a week after the Dundee killings, he'd been pulled from another detective unit to help out the regular homicide investigators, chasing down a random hodgepodge of tips.

Now he would be the only detective solely devoted to this case. But he wouldn't work completely alone. The homicide chief decided Mois would assist Warner. In effect, Mois would be pulling double duty. He still worked his regular night shift in homicide, picking up and investigating new cases. But he would also come in a few hours early most days to chase down Dundee leads.

The pairing of Mois and Warner marked the start of a long and fruitful partnership within Omaha's homicide unit, one that in coming years would see the smart and dedicated duo solve dozens of Omaha killings. When it came to personality, though, the new partners came from opposite poles of the planet.

The son of a Missouri engineering school dean, Warner had a professorial look of his own, with a well-groomed mustache, jowly face and a document bag often slung over his shoulder. Warner was a stickler for the department dress code, always looking squared away in his crisp suits and ties. He'd also just as soon hack off a limb than get a tattoo. "Not my cup of tea," he'd say.

While Mois, like many homicide detectives, swore around the office like a longshoreman, no such words ever crossed Warner's proper lips. Neither man was easily ruffled or excited. But Warner exuded an almost priest-like calm — a demeanor he used to his advantage as one of the department's best interviewers and interrogators.

Around an interrogation room, Warner displayed a practiced patience that was almost inhuman. For most criminals, lying comes as easily as breathing. Warner understood that, accepted it and never got flustered in the least. He'd simply outlast them. Warner could question a subject for hours, hearing nothing but a web of untruth and seemingly getting nowhere. Then just when the subject might think the grilling was finally, mercifully over, Warner would calmly say, "OK, let's start over again. From the very beginning."

It was enough to drive even his fellow detectives mad. But his persistence also frequently produced results. The subject would often slip into an inconsistency. Or perhaps fall victim to Warner's soft, fatherly approach, coming clean like a kindergartner before the school principal.

As the new lead detective, Warner represented a fresh set of eyes for Dundee. He spent hours poring over the crime scene photos, scoping every detail to see if something had been missed. Warner himself was a new father, so the images of the vulnerable Tom really hit home with him. He'd previously heard the killer described as some kind of monster, a madman, a sociopath. From what Warner could see in these pictures, he could be all of those things. Warner wanted badly to see the killer in cuffs.

Mois had teamed up with Warner in the past. But the more he worked with him on Dundee, the more he came to appreciate him. Warner had a reassuring presence about him and clearly knew his stuff. Mois was also delighted to see that inside that starched collar, Warner also had a sense of humor, a clownish side that came out more and more as the detectives worked together. It really wasn't as odd a pairing as it had seemed. They clicked.

Around their desks in homicide, Warner and Mois would spend hours discussing the case. What was most important? What needs more scrutiny? They looked for loose threads and grabbed hold of them. "It occupied our lives every day," Mois would later say. "And when I say every day, I mean every day."

A particular focus of Mois during late 2008 came to be whether Tom could have been the victim of some kind of internet predator. Omaha detectives had seized all the Hunters' electronic devices in the wake of the killings. After sifting through them with the help of the FBI, they saw Tom had been interacting with dozens of people online, both in chat rooms and through online gaming on his Xbox.

Most of these people only appeared as obscure screen names like "iiiifireiiii" or "pockypowah." Through subpoenas sent to Microsoft and website operators, Mois dug deeper. He wanted to learn who the anonymous people were behind the screen names and whether they could have ever had direct contact with Tom. In the end, Mois would literally track these people all over the country and around the globe — as far away as Iraq.

In looking at Tom's online interactions, Mois and other detectives did find some communications that concerned them. Tom had been frequenting a chat room on a popular educational website for pre-teen kids called Whyville. He was sending and receiving messages in this chat room under his screen name "kupcakek." In fact, the night before he died, Tom had been on the site.

As Mois found, things in Whyville weren't always as they seemed. He learned after tracking down a young girl who had befriended Tom on the site that he had represented himself to her as a 17-year-old roughneck, a tough kid who got into fights and had bad grades. But more concerning to Mois was evidence that there were others interacting on the site who were much older than they represented themselves to be. That included at least one college student that Tom had both chatted with on Whyville and played video games with.

Why would a college student be frequenting a website intended for pre-teen kids? And while this college kid was playing video games nearly every day, why did the records Mois obtained show he was curiously offline in the days around the Dundee killings? Mois wanted to learn more.

As the only full-time Dundee investigator, Warner worked lots of different angles. Many times he'd wake at home at 3 a.m. and be struck by an idea. Sometimes he'd follow a lead and get excited for a while, but then days later dismiss it in the face of new evidence. Warner, though, in the end came to particularly focus on one man who for years would be seen as the prime suspect in the Dundee killings.

Just days after the murders, Hunter had sat down at Creighton with Dr. Brumback, the chair of the department, and another senior department administrator. Together they went down a list of every resident who had gone through the Creighton pathology program since the 1990s — dozens of names. Name by name, they talked about all of them. While they dismissed most immediately, there came to be much discussion about one: a Russian doctor who not long before had conflicts with several people in the pathology department.

During his three years at Creighton from 2004 to 2007, the Russian had been variously seen by people in the department as intimidating, odd and creepy. One female staff member felt he had violated her personal space when they stood together. Brumback didn't like the Russian. Brumback had insisted, against Hunter's wishes, that Hunter put him on review and order him to undergo a psychological evaluation. In response, the Russian filed an employment discrimination complaint against the school. What had seemed to Hunter a minor incident had turned into a major fiasco for the department.

Hunter eventually defused the situation. He even helped the Russian land a good job in Pittsburgh that more fit his interests. The Russian seemed generally pleased with how it all worked out, so much so he agreed to drop his complaint against the school.

Given all that, Hunter saw no reason that the Russian would have a beef with him.

But the department's senior administrator, and to a lesser degree Brumback, thought during the meeting that day that the Russian might still hold a grudge against the school. Rumors circulated around Creighton that he even had connections to the Russian mafia. There was also discussion that the Russian looked somewhat like the police sketch.

Talk of the Russian heated up even more, Hunter would recall, when police detectives arrived in the midst of the meeting at Creighton that day.

The detectives seemed interested in the Russian doctor, too. And that was affirmed days later when a group of four detectives came to Hunter's home. That was the same day the Hunters gave their short list of potential suspects to the detectives. In addition to discussing the handful of names the Hunters had listed, the detectives asked many questions about the Russian.

However, when those initial investigators looked into the Russian's background, he seemed to have an alibi. At the time of the killings, he worked in the county coroner's office in Pittsburgh. Records there suggested he was on the job that March day.

Still, Omaha detectives remained skeptical. It wasn't as if the Russian punched a time clock each day. And though he had performed an autopsy the day prior to the killings, he wasn't part of any on March 13. Could he have made his way to Omaha? It seemed there may have been a small window there.

As the new lead investigator, Warner would give the Russian a long, second look.

Warner re-interviewed some Creighton officials and also spoke with new ones. He further probed the employment records in Pittsburgh. And when he felt the time was right, he became the first Omaha detective to confront the Russian face-to-face.

By then, the Russian had left Pittsburgh to take a coroner's job in Calgary, Canada. So traveling with an FBI agent, Warner flew north of the border. It wasn't common for Warner to hop a plane as part of his work. Trying to protect his curious 5-year-old daughter from the gruesome nature of this business trip, Warner told her he was flying off in pursuit of a donut robber. For a long time afterwards, she asked him if they ever caught the guy who stole all those powdered donuts.

Memorably, Warner and the FBI agent landed in Calgary amid a massive snowstorm. To top it off, the airline lost their luggage. So the next day, dressed in the same clothes they'd worn the day before, the investigators dropped in at the Russian's office.

They arrived unannounced. Warner wanted to read the Russian's face and body language when they flashed their badges. And Warner didn't want to give him any opportunity to rehearse answers.

The Russian was clearly surprised but also cordial, agreeing to sit down. Warner spent several hours patiently walking the Russian through his time at Creighton, his relationships with everyone there, and the nature of his departure from the school. He asked about the Russian's discrimination complaint, whether he ever had a conflict with Hunter, whether he'd ever met Hunter's son. Warner already knew the answers to nearly all the questions he was asking. He wanted to see if the Russian slipped.

By the end, Warner still wasn't completely convinced there was no way the Russian could have been in Omaha on March 13, 2008. But as he boarded the plane to return to Nebraska, Warner's gut told him the Russian just had no motive to harm Dr. Hunter or his child.

Exhaust a lead. Move on to the next best one. That was the life of a homicide investigator. Warner thought of where he would turn next. But Warner soon learned this was actually the end of the line in Dundee for both he and Mois. Their bosses decided Dundee had essentially gone cold. And that was underscored when in early 2009 the Omaha police leadership administratively transferred the case to the department's cold case unit.

Mois understood the decision. He knew that cold case, with some of the department's top detectives specifically dedicated to dormant cases, would be able to put resources behind Dundee. But at the same time, he was frustrated by his superiors' call.

He felt Dundee detectives from the start had been too often side-tracked by bureaucratic meddling, asked to chase the latest random tip down some rabbit hole. Mois recalled the time a caller suggested there was someone at a mall who looked like the man in the sketch. Mois was told to drop what he was doing to canvass the mall — in his mind a complete and maddening waste of time.

Mois also didn't agree that the case had gone cold. He and Warner still had not run out of leads. Mois was still exploring the background of the college kid who had been interacting with Tom online. He hadn't even gotten to the point of interviewing him yet. "I'm not done," Mois said.

What gnawed at Mois most was the simple fact they had not been able to crack this case. Both he and Warner felt badly they'd been unable to bring some peace to the Hunter and Waite families. "I don't care who solves it," Warner said. "I just want it solved."

Still grieving their losses, the world turned a little more slowly for the Hunter and Waite families. March 13, 2009 — the one-year anniversary of the Dundee killings — passed without an arrest. Friends and neighbors of the Hunters marked the anniversary with a solemn candlelight vigil around the Hunters' front porch. Both families despaired that the case would never be solved. "It is just killing us as a family, not knowing who or why," Bill Hunter told an *Omaha World-Herald* reporter. "Obviously, we are desperately seeking closure."

While Dundee was now housed in the cold case unit, police officials publicly emphasized that didn't mean it was going into cold storage. The unit had been created by the department the year before specifically to work on these types of high-profile, unsolved cases. And Lt. Ken Kanger, the hard-driving cop who headed the unit, was bound and determined to solve Dundee.

In the months and years to come, Kanger would have his detectives pore through the files and re-interview past witnesses. They had the Hunters again consider anyone at Creighton who could have done it. Detectives visited Tom's friends as they grew up and matured, just to see if they had held anything back. And the detectives continued to go through old tips. While the unit also worked other cases, Dundee never sat on a shelf. Rarely did a week or month go by without the unit chasing down something.

Cold case eventually did interview the college kid on Whyville that Mois was so interested in. He, too, was cleared. The online predator theory also became a major theme when the case was featured in a 2012 episode of the *"America's Most Wanted"* TV show. Omaha police cooperated with the producers, still looking for that elusive tip that could blow the case wide open.

Cold case also continued to dig into the Russian, finally finding what appeared to be an ironclad alibi for him. Computer records they obtained through a search warrant showed an email had been sent from his desk in Pittsburgh just hours before the Omaha murders.

As the time passed, Shirlee's family grew increasingly frustrated. They were bothered by the turnover of detectives on the case. And to Shirlee's family, resorting to a TV show proved police were lost and totally grasping.

But the Waites also didn't easily give up. Not only did the family contribute significantly to the reward fund, they also spent $20,000 for a private detective to do his own probing around the case. The private eye particularly looked hard at Creighton connections, which the Waite family had become convinced were the key to the murders. Their investigator also became much interested in the Russian, not at all convinced he was in the clear. But try as he might, the private eye couldn't place the Russian in Omaha, either.

Time marched on. By the end of 2012 — nearly five years after the Dundee slayings — the Omaha police files on the case filled seven 4-inch binders, a stack of paper some two feet high. All that work. All that effort. And yet Omaha detectives were still no closer to identifying the mysterious man in the silver SUV, the ruthless killer who so brazenly walked Dundee's quiet streets that day.

The difficulty in solving Dundee had been particularly underscored late in 2008. That's when the FBI's behavioral science unit had come out with its insights into the case. To make sure detectives weren't missing anything, Mois about two months into the Dundee investigation had engaged with the famed FBI behavioral unit, based in Quantico, Virginia.

The FBI ran details of the case through a computer database that looked for similar crimes committed around the country. It was hoped the unusual nature of the knives left in the necks would point to a related crime elsewhere. An FBI official also flew out from Washington to get more details and to personally walk the crime scene.

The psychological profile that the agency produced in the end didn't offer the magical insight Mois had been hoping for. It wasn't anything like what you see on TV, where such a report would suggest the killer was a 28-year-old white male who lives in his mom's basement and likes cats. The conclusions were far more general.

There was at least one intriguing suggestion in the FBI profile: that the culprit was a serial-killing drifter. The prospect they were dealing with a serial killer certainly had not been lost on the Omaha detectives. Mois, though, also knew that suggestion and $5 would get you a Starbucks latte. It didn't really bring detectives any closer to the killer.

But in the end, the FBI profile would prove prophetic in another way. It suggested police would likely not find him until he killed again.

CHAPTER 7: MOTHER'S DAY

Just past daybreak, Mother's Day 2013, Mary Brumback awoke to a pleasant surprise.

Son Owen Brumback was on early-morning dad duty with his daughter, Savannah. And the 6-month-old was sleepless in suburban Denver.

So Owen — the tall, thin, blonde-haired son of Dr. Roger and Mary Brumback — dialed up his mom in Omaha. He loved calling his mom — and did so several times a week, just to chat. "I like to talk; she likes to talk," Owen would later say. "I just wanted to keep her company. I liked talking to her."

Owen decided to turn this Mother's Day into Grandmother's Day. He told his mom to switch over to FaceTime so she and Roger could see their granddaughter in all her gum-toothed glory.

Savannah smiled and cooed and drooled and did all the cute things that a 6-month-old does. Sitting in front of their iPad, the Brumbacks beamed. A week before, they had been to Denver to visit Owen and wife Chrissy and see Savannah's baptism. It was a near-perfect, extended weekend with family. But on Mother's Day, this FaceTime call would prove short-lived. After Savannah got squirmy, Owen wished Mom a Happy Mother's Day and hung up.

With that kick start, the Brumbacks went about their Sunday. All around the house on this beautiful May 12 in Omaha were signs of a couple on the verge of their next adventure:

retirement. An empty hutch, its drawers barren. Computers, aligned and unplugged. Boxes packed, marked and stacked. The couple, both 65, had decided to move to West Virginia, where both would be closer to relatives. So several weeks before, Roger had announced he would leave his workplace of the past 12-plus years — the pathology department at Creighton medical school.

Brumback, a native of Pittsburgh, had started his four-decade medical career in 1967. A brilliant young prodigy, at age 19 he became the youngest student in the very first class of Penn State's new medical school in Hershey, Pennsylvania. After a distinguished academic and medical career that saw him lead Creighton's pathology department for a decade, write or edit 14 books, pen another 130 journal articles, launch and edit two medical journals, and even discover a monkey species, Roger had decided to retire. Sort of.

He had taken an administrative post at the West Virginia School of Osteopathic Medicine, a college in Lewisburg, West Virginia that focuses on natural healing. Evidence-based alternative healing had piqued Brumback's interest late in his life. The rest of his career had been devoted to child neurology and pathology, including his long-time research into Alzheimer's.

Also, during this so-called retirement, the "certifiable workaholic" — as one friend described him — planned to continue to edit his two journals, one in child neurology and the other in alternative medicine. "I think Roger's idea of retirement was cutting back from 70 hours a week to 50," a friend, Dr. E. Steve Roach, said. "Roger was one of those rare people who was very nice to people, very, very smart and worked very hard."

The same could be said for Mary Brumback. A pleasant woman with a wisp of white hair, Mary became a pharmacist after graduating from Penn State. But she soon chose to go to law school. She later pursued a career in family law while Roger practiced and taught at the University of Oklahoma College of Medicine in Norman. The couple, who met in college, wrote a book on dietary fiber and weight control, and Mary helped Roger launch and edit the *Journal of Child Neurology*.

When Roger took over Creighton's pathology department in 2001, Mary gave up the legal world, channeling her detail-oriented mind into other pursuits. She worked at a hospital gift shop and also volunteered through a philanthropic educational organization at Creighton.

Mary also ran the Brumback house. A prolific communicator, she talked to her sons, Daryl and Owen, all the time. She also spoke daily to her mother or her caregivers at her nursing home, dutifully keeping a journal documenting these talks and her mother's care. "Told her I went to service league luncheon at Donna Foley's and got our mower back," she'd written two days earlier. "She seemed fine mentally — not agitated, not confused."

Mary saved her most extensive prose for her daughter, Dr. Audrey Brumback. Every week, without fail, Audrey would get a letter from her mother. Long-form, cursive writing. Thoughtful. Detailed.

The only daughter of the Brumbacks had followed in her father's footsteps, pursuing a career in child neurology. Dad and daughter would often talk business — updating each other on advancements in their chosen science.

As for mom, Audrey shared her mother's funny-feisty streak. It was abundant as Audrey years later recounted the weekly ritual they shared. Audrey would go to the mailbox and retrieve the stationery-sized envelope with her mother's smooth handwriting. Then she would announce to her husband: "Oh, the Mary Brumback letter came today!"

"It was awesome — I'd get one every week," she'd ruefully recall later. "Fifty-two letters a year ... from my mom."

This Mother's Day, though, Audrey Brumback chose a more modern form of communication. Like her brother, she contacted her parents from her home in San Francisco via FaceTime. It was early afternoon. And for an hour and 4 minutes, Roger and Mary talked with their daughter. Audrey caught up on life and the move and weather and Mother's Day.

At one point, Audrey razzed her mom about giving unsolicited advice to Audrey's husband. Audrey said she knew the crack would get a laugh — "I'm hilarious," she quipped — so she grabbed a screenshot of her parents' reaction to her words. In the photo, Roger pulls away from the iPad, as if to give himself room to bellow. Mary is beet red, mid-laugh at her daughter's zinger.

It was the last image of the couple alive.

* * *

The Brumbacks weren't the only ones on the cusp of retirement that gorgeous Mother's Day. Againdra and Chhanda Bewtra were approaching the twilight of their careers at Creighton. And they, too, were celebrating the holiday as empty nesters. The Bewtras went to a midtown Omaha restaurant to have lunch with their close friends, retired college professor Richard Thill and his wife, Florence.

Chhanda Bewtra, a professor and pathologist who worked alongside Roger Brumback and Bill Hunter at Creighton, and Againdra Bewtra, himself a doctor at Creighton, were a contagiously outgoing couple who constantly talked over each other. Thill and his wife also weren't bashful. So lunch went long. And then afterwards the couples walked toward their cars.

At the time, Thill was using a walker to get around. The departure from the restaurant was painfully slow. So slow that Againdra ribbed Thill. "Richard!" he said in the accent of his native India. "You are really causing us delays!"

The delay would be fortuitous. In fact, it may have saved the Bewtras' lives.

After the Bewtras drove away, no more than two minutes from their home near 84th and Pacific Streets, their home security system sent an alert to their cell phones. An alarm had been triggered at 2:16 p.m. Againdra Bewtra soon after pulled into the driveway, not sure if it was a false alarm. Just to be sure, he asked his wife to stay back in the car as he checked it out.

The diminutive man — his driver's license lists him at a generous 5 feet, 6 inches tall — walked the perimeter of his house. Then he checked the monitor in the home to see which of the sensors had tripped.

Bewtra ultimately found that someone had tried to push in the locked French doors in the back of the house, budging them about two inches. The break-in attempt had been thwarted by the second piece of low-tech security equipment Againdra Bewtra had installed: a large recliner-couch that he had jammed against the inside of the doors. "It would take superhuman strength to move that thing," Againdra would later say, spreading his hands and arms like a pro wrestler.

The Bewtras didn't think much of the alarm, declining to report it to police. After all, nothing had been taken.

Turns out, this had not been just a burglar at their back door.

CHAPTER 8: CHANGE OF PLANS

The stranger in the black Mercedes SUV drove east on Pacific Street, surely charged with both adrenaline and frustration. That door that refused to budge had foiled his latest attempt to seek revenge against the people in his past who did him wrong. Bewtra. Bitch had it coming.

Now he didn't know where he was going exactly. He was only vaguely familiar with Omaha. He'd once lived there for about a year, but that had been a long, long time ago. In the interim, he had made a brief return trip to the city. That visit, some five years earlier, had been one neither he nor most anyone in Omaha would soon forget.

He drove on, still buzzing from the case of beer he'd picked up across the river in Iowa an hour earlier. Every day anymore, he pretty much woke up drunk and never stopped drinking. As he neared 72nd Street, he saw a sign that pierced his foggy brain. "Wingstop," it said in big green letters. A chicken wing joint.

That suddenly looked good. Borderline morbidly obese at 5-foot-8 and more than 270 pounds, he usually wasn't one to miss a meal. He'd prefer a Hooters, the restaurant chain that featured three of his favorite things in all the world: wings, beer and scantily clad women. But in a pinch, this would do. He turned into the parking lot and lumbered inside.

Standing below the counter sign which proclaimed Wingstop "the Wing Experts," he scanned the menu board and placed his order. At 2:26 p.m., he used one of his many overworked credit cards to pay the $7.69 tab.

A half hour later, he was back in the Mercedes, parked right out front. He pulled out his iPhone. The homicidal thoughts, irrationality and desperation that had recently driven him continued to spin in a menacing whirlwind through his head.

Perhaps he could still find a way salvage this trip after all. Opening up the phone's tiny keyboard, with thick fingers he typed a name into the browser:

r-o-g-e-r b-r-u-m-b-a-c-k.

A Whitepages entry came up, giving the home address for Dr. Roger Brumback. It was near 114th and Shirley Streets. Conveniently, it even wasn't far away, the map showing it just a few miles west on Pacific Street.

This stop had been a pretty good call. He shifted his car into drive and soon was headed west again, fueled by both the wings and his deadly new purpose.

* * *

Roger and Mary Brumback weren't expecting Mother's Day guests. They had just finished that FaceTime call with Audrey. And their house was now littered with signs of the laidback Sunday they'd spent together.

On the kitchen table: a rock propped open a romance novel that Mary had been reading. Omaha's Sunday newspaper had been pulled apart, its sections akimbo.

Roger had gathered dozens of his old medical books and piled them in his car trunk, ready to donate them to a Des Moines college the next day. It's just a two-hour trip from Omaha to Des Moines, but Mary had convinced Roger that the couple needed to make a day of it in the Iowa city — shop and dine and do things that semi-retired couples do.

In the meantime, there was work to be done to get the house ready to sell. Wearing a dark shirt, shorts and old leather loafers, Roger was giving the foyer a fresh coat of paint. A ladder — a gallon of paint underneath it — sat in the front hallway. Roger had no idea what was lurking just outside on this sun-splashed, tranquil, 68-degree day.

Someone knocked or rang at the Brumbacks' door. Roger opened the white wooden main door to find a heavyset man in a blue dress shirt and black slacks standing there.

It's impossible to know what was in Brumback's mind at the moment. He may have originally thought it was a door-to-door salesman — someone to politely shoo away. Or a proselytizer, taking his gospel into people's homes. Or perhaps Brumback immediately recognized this man from his past, a man who was carrying a festering, 12-year-old grudge. Either way, it appears Brumback had little time to think or talk about it. Because the visitor pulled out a Smith & Wesson SD9 semiautomatic pistol.

Brumback and the avenger began struggling over the gun right there on the door's threshold. The life-and-death battle tripped the gun's magazine release, the shiny gold ammunition clip clunking down right in the doorway. But not before the assailant first squeezed off three shots. They rang out into the neighborhood, breaking the Mother's Day solitude.

One bullet struck Brumback in the lower leg. Another passed through his shoulder and the wooden door behind him before lodging in the drywall above a closet. The other, the fatal one, was an odd, upward-angled shot that ripped through his abdomen and struck his liver and a blood vessel before lodging in his back. Brumback fell back heavily to the wooden floor of the entryway, landing in a near-fetal position.

After hearing shots fired, Mary must have rushed to the entryway, finding her husband on the floor, his assailant standing over him. She, too, soon was struggling with the gunman, her glasses falling to the floor near her dying husband.

With no clip, the gun was now inoperable. So the man turned it to more primitive use, viciously pistol-whipping Mary. He hammered her across the forehead so hard the gun actually broke.

Mary must have been dazed by the head blow, which left a large gash on her forehead. The temporary incapacitation allowed the attacker to turn to other means to finish her off. Familiar, sadistic means.

He went into the kitchen. He first pulled open what turned out to be a junk drawer. Then he found what he'd come looking for in the drawer right next to it. There amid a pile of kitchen utensils he spied the knives. He grabbed two of them, in the process leaving a tiny drop of Mary's blood on the counter. The little red blot would later help detectives piece together the tale of violence inside the Brumbacks' home that day.

Knives in hand, the assailant returned to the living room. If Mary had been woozy from the blow to her head, seeing this man now brandishing the blades must have gotten her full attention. Because as a prosecutor would later put it, "She fought with every fiber she had in her."

With her bare hands, the 65-year-old desperately warded off slash after slash from the knife-wielding killer, enduring what had to be extremely painful wounds. She would suffer more than 20 cuts to her hands and arms.

One slash carved a deep, 3-inch slit completely through her right wrist, the knife coming out the other side. At another point, she held up her left hand to block the knife. The result: Her left thumb was nearly severed — hacked all the way through the joint, attached only by a tendon. Mary's blood flew all around — on to walls, boxes, tables and furniture, the teardrop-shaped stains later telling the story of Mary's bitter struggle.

Ultimately, Mary could ward off the assault no more, the assailant able to fight his way in close and subdue her. He plunged the knife repeatedly into the right side of her neck, just below her ear and jaw line. An autopsy would later reveal the blade hit its intended target — severing her carotid artery.

Then the killer walked slowly back over to Roger. The leisurely pace of his stroll would later be forensically revealed by the trail of Mary's blood that fell off the knife blade to the floor in perfectly round droplets.

Roger in all likelihood was already dead or near-dead as he lay slumped in the entryway. That would later be proven by the clean and orderly knife wounds left in his neck, contrasting to the half-dozen jagged ones left in the neck of his desperately struggling wife. No matter. Just to be sure he'd finished the job — and to leave his familiar, grisly mark — the killer six times plunged the blade into the right side of Roger's neck, severing his carotid artery.

The killer then walked back to Mary, dropped the knife to the floor and rolled her over to make sure she, too, was dead. He could see his brutal work was done here.

Just like five years earlier, the mystery man's visit to Omaha had not gone exactly as planned. For the second time, two people were left dead who weren't his true, intended targets. Nonetheless, with his horrid deeds, he felt he'd again achieved a measure of vengeance, the price to be paid for the sabotaging of his career. In his twisted world view, they had brought this on themselves.

He climbed back into his Mercedes. Pulling out his phone again, he looked up where he could jump on the nearest freeway. He picked up Interstate 80, the cross-country freeway running through the city, and headed east for home.

In the Brumback home, blood silently pooled beneath the butchered couple, leaving a spot on the carpet beneath Mary the size of a manhole cover. Mary's lifeless body lay just feet away from a small desk that was topped by a smiling 8-by-10 portrait of her beloved husband, his professional mug shot from early Creighton days.

Also atop the desk was a promotional folder for the moving company the Brumbacks had hired to ship their life belongings to their new home in West Virginia. On its front, in large letters:

"Life never stops moving."

CHAPTER 9: 'HE'S BACK'

Derek Mois ducked his head and shoulder under a strand of yellow police tape and strode toward the front door of the white, black-shuttered suburban home. The veteran homicide detective didn't have a lot to go on at this point, only the initial officer's report that there were two unknown deceased parties inside, an older man and woman.

Mois talked to the uniformed officer standing guard by the door, securing the crime scene. She pointed out across the way to a group of piano movers, one of whom had earlier placed the original 911 call.

On this Tuesday morning May 14 — two days after Mother's Day — Jason Peterson and his two-man piano-moving crew had come to the house with a work order to haul away a no-longer-needed upright. Peterson had been curious when he got no answer after he repeatedly rang and knocked. And then he got downright suspicious when he pulled open the unlocked door to call out to anyone inside. That's when he spotted a handgun magazine sitting on the threshold. He immediately told his crew to back off. Then he called the cops.

"I just think there's something going on in this house," he told the 911 operator. He was right. The first uniformed officer on the scene found a ghastly spectacle inside.

Mois and his partners all had the same initial thought when the first officer's findings were called into the homicide bureau: a murder/suicide. They were basing that mostly on the home's location in this serene, wooded and pricey subdivision, and the fact there were two bodies down, a man and a woman. They'd seen lots of past cases in nice neighborhoods where a lover's quarrel ended with someone pulling a gun and then violently ending the relationship — as well as two lives. Or sometimes with an older couple like these victims, it was just a case of one or both deciding they were done living. But you never know. Mois was prepared for anything.

In the five years since he'd worked the 2008 Dundee murder case, much had changed for Mois. In fact, it wasn't at all a given he'd still be working homicide, let alone showing up at this gruesome crime scene.

Mois had actually left homicide in 2009, finally deciding the 24/7 on-call demands and piles of extra hours were putting too much strain on his young family. He'd missed his son's first Christmas. He'd missed family birthday parties. He'd canceled vacations. There were just too many moments and milestones he would never get back.

He transferred to a unit investigating other major crimes like bank robberies and rapes. Home life was more peaceful. But Mois also found the work just wasn't the same.

It wasn't long before Mois was begging the homicide lieutenant to take him back. He missed the challenge. He missed the special unit camaraderie that only those in homicide truly understood. "I knew I had to get back to those guys and those cases," he'd later say. By 2011, he pounced on an opening and transferred back. This bloody work really does get into your blood. He knew it was part of him now.

Mois' return to homicide was eased by the fact the unit had a new lieutenant, a mother hen who was big on family-life balance and well-attuned to the needs of her detectives. To ease the personal demands, Lt. Stefanie Fidone had reconstructed the dozen-detective unit to create three teams of four detectives. Most critically with the new set-up, only one of the three teams would be on call at any given time. That meant that unless his team was the next one up in rotation, Mois could go to sleep at night or go out to watch his kids' ball games without fear of suddenly being called away.

Mois and other veteran detectives also came to see the change as far more conducive to successful investigations. With this system, all members of the team became intimate with every detail of their cases, regularly briefing as a group, working as a true team, and sticking with each case to the end. To Mois, it sure beat the scatter-shot way detectives were assigned to cases in the past.

Some detectives would later believe the Dundee investigation had suffered under the old way of business. Frontline investigators weren't all on the same page and didn't have the full picture. At best, maybe a sergeant had the details of what detectives collectively knew. There were too many opportunities for information to be lost in translation, never shared or forgotten.

As it happened, Mois' team was next in line for this May 2013 call. So just as he had with Dundee five years earlier, he would handle the crime scene here. It was a fortuitous coincidence — one that would become particularly meaningful not long after Mois walked through the front door.

Mois had arrived with two other members from his four-detective team: Warner, his old partner dating back to Dundee, and detective Ryan Davis, the team's newest member. The team's fourth, Nick Herfordt, stayed back downtown after taking the initial call. He handled the paperwork needed to secure the search warrant so detectives could start combing through the home.

That warrant was now in hand. So while Davis immediately set off to canvas the neighborhood for witnesses, Mois and Warner walked past the ramp the piano movers had set up on the front steps and got their first look inside.

The detectives were careful not to disturb the handgun magazine, which was right on the threshold as they'd been warned. Mois also immediately spotted other things, including a single shell casing lying not far from the clip and a bullet hole in the main door.

Stepping into the entryway, the detectives were greeted by the smell of death. It was clear the victims had not been killed this day. After the detectives' eyes adjusted to the dim indoor light, they spied the first body, lying right in front of them. The body of the second victim was also visible from where they stood, off to the left in the living room.

And there was blood. An enormous amount of blood, in wide pools and scattered in droplets on the floor, furniture and walls. Mois could already see this was no murder/suicide. These victims had lost their lives in a frenzied fight to the death.

To Mois, it seemed the first victim had been accosted at the front door and shot right there. Mois immediately noticed the apparent gunshot wounds visible through the man's clothes. But there were also vicious stab wounds to the side of his neck. It looked to Mois like whoever shot this man wanted to make sure he was dead. This was no casual killing. This was personal.

The victim had fallen amid painting supplies, an aluminum ladder and boxes stacked in the hall, signs, it seemed, of a family in the midst of a move. The piano those movers had been coming to fetch was just beyond the first victim's head.

Mois and Warner drifted off to the left towards the second body. But before they got there, Mois came upon more gun parts. Kind of a gun nut, Mois recognized these pieces right away. There was the inner recoil spring and rod from a semiautomatic handgun. There was also a U-shaped piece of metal, part of the gun's frame that had broken off. He figured that fracture was why the gun had broken, causing those other pieces to fall to the floor.

Not far away on the cream and orange carpet was a knife, a wood-handled kitchen knife with a weathered handle, brass rivets and tarnished blade. And as Mois stood over the female victim, he saw a similar blade beneath her. This one was bloodied, apparently the one used to kill her.

Whoever this woman was, Mois could also see she had fought off that knife with every ounce of life she had. Blood had been propelled in all directions. Mois recognized the many defensive wounds on her hands and arms. The woman had also suffered an obvious bludgeoning wound near the top of her head. Mois then saw what appeared to be the fatal wounds: a series of major cuts to the right side of her neck.

Eyeing this crime scene for the first time, Mois and Warner were noticing some things that were immediately familiar to them. A pair of victims. In a beautiful home. Valuables all around, with no sign of theft. And most notably, knife wounds to the sides of their necks. Warner would even recall the two detectives exchanged a couple of knowing looks as they soft-shoed their way through the carnage. They'd worked together enough that they didn't have to say it aloud. But a thought was already flickering. Could it be? "I've seen these things before," Mois would recall thinking.

Their tour of the home then took them into the adjoining kitchen, where they saw two drawers had been pulled open. One was the ubiquitous junk drawer. Every house, Mois knew, has a kitchen junk drawer, the place you put scissors, rubber bands, pens, batteries, flashlights, old bills, keys of long-forgotten origin and anything else that doesn't have a home.

It was the other open drawer, though, that stood out. That one was filled with a jumble of kitchen utensils and gadgets, cheese graters, egg beaters, whisks and the like. But most noticeable to Mois were the knives. Kitchen knives with faded wooden handles, brass rivets and tarnished blades. Knives exactly like the ones used on these victims. Suddenly there were alarms sounding in the detectives' heads. Stab wounds to the neck delivered with knives taken right from the home.

When Mois and Warner finished their initial walk through and stepped outside, they held an aside. "God, I hope this isn't what it looks like," Mois said. No kidding, Warner replied. The two talked about the striking similarities between these killings and the Dundee slayings five years earlier. It's not as if they were convinced at the moment the pairs of deaths were related. You see a lot weird stuff in homicide. But they'd already observed so much, it seemed kind of eerie.

It took a phone call from downtown minutes later to convince the detectives that what they were seeing wasn't just some strange coincidence.

Herfordt, the other detective on Mois' team, was still at the office. He was anxious to get out to the crime scene but was begrudgingly doing more paperwork, he and homicide Sgt. Sheila Cech trying to determine the possible identities of the victims in the house. Cech looked online at county property records and found the registered owner of the house: Roger A. Brumback. To get a better idea of who he was, she simply typed his name into Google.

Among the top results popping up on her screen was one for a Dr. Roger A. Brumback, M.D. It showed he was a physician affiliated with Creighton University's medical center. Digging further, Cech determined that Brumback had been a department chairman at Creighton: the pathology department.

It was like a bolt of lightning. Cech instantly knew the potential significance of her finding. In fact, years later, Herfordt recalled Cech's words as she turned to him from her computer screen.

"He's back."

CHAPTER 10: SERIAL KILLER AT LARGE

Mois and Warner were still barely into their work at the Brumback crime scene when Lt. Fidone relayed the word from Herfordt downtown. For the first time, Mois learned of the victims' Creighton pathology link.

"Wait, this is Roger Brumback, and he works at Creighton in pathology? That's what you're telling me?" Mois said as he huddled with his boss.

"It sure looks like it," Fidone replied. "This is his house."

"OK, we've got a problem," Mois said. "We've already made observations here that are extremely similar to Dundee. They are significant."

With the signature knife wounds and Creighton connection, it didn't take a criminal justice degree for anyone to realize these latest killings could well be linked to Dundee.

It was also clear what they now needed to do. The detectives decided that Warner would immediately break away and begin exploring the ties between Brumback and Hunter. By 2 p.m., Warner was on the phone with Bill Hunter, telling him there was a high probability the two cases were linked. By 5:30 p.m., Warner and a whole team of detectives were at Hunter's front door, some six miles away from the Brumback house.

Bill Hunter had been floored to learn of Brumback's death, hearing of it after Brumback failed to show up to deliver a scheduled parting lecture at Creighton the same day the bodies were discovered. Hunter in his gut now knew there almost had to be a Creighton tie to the killing of his son — something he'd always found impossible to grasp. But he still couldn't think of what, or who, it was.

The investigators talked with Hunter for hours, learning about his now-deceased former boss and anyone in his orbit. Were there any students or staff members with a possible grudge against both Hunter and Brumback? They went over the Russian again. The Russian's major beef had actually been with Brumback. So in the minds of Warner and the other detectives, he was definitely back on the radar. Hunter also mentioned a couple of residents who had been fired more than a decade earlier after a prank against a fellow resident. It had been so long Hunter couldn't recall the name of one of the students.

As crime scene lead, Mois continued his work at the Brumback house — he would spend three days there — and again attended the victims' autopsies. By now he had already followed the trail of blood droplets, gun parts and open drawers to piece together the likely sequence of events in the Brumback home: Roger accosted and shot at the door, the clip falling out of the gun in the struggle. Mary coming to her husband's aid. The bludgeoning with the inoperable gun, which breaks. Knives taken from the kitchen, the killer leaving a drop of Mary's blood behind. Mary's desperate, futile fight to fend off the knife. The coup de grace knifings of both victims.

Mois and other detectives also quickly determined the Brumbacks had died two days earlier, on Mother's Day. Talking to the Brumbacks' children, they learned the victims were clad in the same clothes they'd been wearing during their Mother's Day video chats with their kids.

Additionally, Ryan Davis' neighborhood canvas had revealed a neighbor around the corner who reported hearing possible gunshots coming from the direction of the Brumback home on Mother's Day. Since it had been the middle of the day in a neighborhood that was typically a no-fly zone for gunfire, the neighbor had just assumed it was a lawnmower backfiring. The approximate time he heard the shots — just after 3:30 in the afternoon — gave investigators a pretty good idea when the attack had occurred.

As in the Dundee murders, detectives would once again find the killer had gotten in and out of the house without leaving any physical evidence, no fingerprints or DNA on the knives or anywhere else. It buttressed for Mois what he had suspected five years earlier in Dundee: that the killer wore gloves as he worked.

Perhaps they were medical gloves. Indeed, now that there seemed a heightened possibility the killings were related to Creighton's medical school, that offered an obvious possible explanation for why all four victims were cut in the same way. Certainly a medical professional could know how lethal that would be.

Despite such speculation, the potential Creighton pathology connection did not completely steer the investigation. Detectives still had to be open to all possibilities. But the Creighton link to the killings only grew the next day, Wednesday. That's when Herfordt answered the phone in the homicide unit. On the other end of the line was a man, speaking in an accented and apologetic tone.

"I don't want to bother you guys," said Dr. Againdra Bewtra. "It's probably nothing. I'm embarrassed to even be calling you."

Bewtra proceeded to tell Herfordt about his wife's work in Creighton's pathology department with Drs. Hunter and

Brumback. And then about the Mother's Day burglar alarm at their home.

Bewtra told Herfordt he and his wife still saw the incident as probably nothing. But others at Creighton were adamant they should call police. It was a good thing. Herfordt and Fidone certainly saw the significance of this call.

Fidone immediately dispatched detective Oscar Dieguez to interview the Bewtras and check out their home. In what would months later prove a critical move, Dieguez also had a crime lab technician swab the back door for possible DNA.

With this latest development, the detectives added it all up. Not only were there now double-homicides in the homes of a pair of Creighton pathologists, another Creighton pathologist had an apparent break-in at her home about an hour before the Brumback killings — what Chhanda Bewtra would later refer to as "a very close shave."

The news of the Bewtra break-in was suppressed by Omaha police, no burglary report going public. But as it was, Omaha and its news media were already buzzing about the Creighton link between Roger Brumback and Bill Hunter. This was the most sensational crime story in the city in years. While police officials were careful not to publicly fuel such speculation with the bare-bones information they put out for release, behind the scenes even they now had to acknowledge the truth.

There was a serial killer at work in Omaha. And he was targeting Creighton University pathologists.

CHAPTER 11: THE TASK FORCE

The dozens of reporters and photographers chattering in the auditorium of Omaha police headquarters fell silent when Chief Todd Schmaderer entered the room. Standing behind a podium, historical photos of Omaha officers who had fallen in the line of duty as his backdrop, the chief announced he was forming a multi-agency task force that would probe the recent Brumback killings and possible links to the 2008 Dundee murders.

There was urgency in Schmaderer's voice. He had visited Creighton days earlier, seeing the terror in the eyes of the pathology department staff. They were extremely shaken by Brumback's death and the suspected ties to the Hunter murders five years earlier. There was palpable fear that any of them could be next.

The chief said he understood "the fear and the anxiety in the community right now." But there was confidence in his tone, too. He said the resources behind the task force were formidable. "I would not want this task force coming after me," the chief declared.

Schmaderer, 41, was still new to this job, having risen to the rank of chief only the previous year. But the 17-year department veteran had already been impressing both rank-and-file cops and others in the community with his problem-solving skills, savvy decision-making and ever-calm demeanor. Schmaderer wasn't a suit-and-tie kind of chief, coming to work most days in the same sharp, crisp blues the beat cops wore. That's just how he was dressed when he stood before the media that day.

Coming six days after the discovery of the Brumbacks' bodies, Schmaderer's confident words were meant to assure an uneasy public. But they also masked a fear.

If there was a serial killer at large, Schmaderer believed there was a very real possibility he could strike again. The chief wanted to make him think twice about that. "We always felt he was in a very acute state of mind," Schmaderer would recall years later. "We felt the next killing could occur at any time."

Before going to the podium, though, Schmaderer had chosen his words carefully. For while the chief wanted to send the killer a message, he didn't want to provoke him, either. Those who watched Schmaderer that day had no idea of the linguistic tightrope he was walking.

As outlined by the chief, the 21-member task force would be led by Deputy Chief Mary Newman, a top department administrator with decades of experience in criminal investigations. She would be assisted by detective bureau Capt. Kerry Neumann and homicide lieutenant Fidone. A dozen of Omaha's top detectives would work under them, including Mois, Warner, Herfordt and Davis. There would also be direct outside assistance, with both the Nebraska State Patrol and FBI providing detectives.

The FBI's role in the case was significant. The agency had been active in Dundee from the beginning. But the FBI now officially classified the case in its parlance as a 306: a serial murder investigation.

In the FBI's rules of engagement, that had meaning. Under federal laws controlling the FBI's jurisdiction, the designation allowed the agency to bring additional federal assets and powers to the local case, including the ability to place suspects under interstate surveillance. "Due to the similar manner of these homicides and the link between four of the victims with Creighton, there exists the strong possibility these murders were committed by the same subject," read an internal FBI memo authorizing the agency's participation.

The task force set up in a former conference room on the sixth floor of police headquarters. Windows into the conference room were covered over with white paper, Schmaderer making it clear he didn't want internal leaks or rumors to jeopardize the investigation. Computers were brought in. A smart board against a wall listed the latest assignments and to-dos. Over time, the other walls would fill with colorful pictures, maps, flow-charts and other work products.

The task force would be free to go wherever the facts led. But from the start, Schmaderer and Newman outlined several points they wanted addressed.

No. 1 was clearly Creighton. With the pathology department link to the crimes, the Omaha detectives this time subpoenaed all of the department's personnel records —something they did not do during the Dundee investigation five years earlier. Two detectives went to Creighton and started copying personnel files for all employees in the department dating back to 2000, just before Brumback arrived. "We need to look at everybody there," Newman said.

In addition, the task force was tasked with giving a fresh look at all the Dundee suspects. That included Shirlee's daughter's boyfriend, the suspect in the 2007 case where a knife was left in the victim's neck, and, of course, the Russian. Where were they when the Brumbacks were killed? Did they have alibis?

On that front, Warner was the natural choice to get back on the trail of the Russian. In fact, before Warner was even ready to contact the Russian, the detective was in for a surprise.

Just hours into the investigation, the Russian actually called him.

The Russian told Warner he had heard about Brumback's murder. Anticipating Warner's interest, he asked whether the detective wanted to interview him again. And though the Russian insisted he had nothing to do with Brumback's death, he intriguingly professed to not being particularly unhappy that Brumback was now dead. There was indeed a grudge there. Given this phone call, Warner now had to wonder whether he was dealing with a serial killer who was playing mind games with him. It was all very strange.

Other assignments were handed out, not all of them as sexy as tracking the embittered Russian. There were lots of routine checks that needed to be made. No task was too big or too small. This was not a time for egos.

In that light, Derek Mois received his initial assignment from the task force: talking to friends and acquaintances of Mary Brumback. Was there anything in her background that could make her a target? Was it possible she and Roger had marital problems? Any other skeletons in their closets? It might not have seemed the most promising of avenues for finding a serial killer. But Mois also knew it was nitty-gritty detective work that must be done.

During his casing of the crime scene, Mois had seen papers on Mary's desk showing she was involved with Creighton's chapter of the PEO Sisterhood, a worldwide charity seeking to advance women's place in education. Mois tracked down a number of Mary's PEO sisters and arranged to sit down with them for interviews.

Collectively, these women were some of the kindest, most considerate do-gooders Mois had met in his life. And all the PEO sisters described themselves as extremely close to Mary — almost like real sisters. If there was anything unusual going on in her life, each of them said, I would know about it.

In the end, Mois did hear one familiar refrain from the PEO sisters: speculation that the killer had to be "that crazy Russian doctor." But the PEO sisters also had nothing to back their belief. When it came to evidence that would actually help solve Mary's murder, these interviews were getting Mois nowhere fast.

On May 27, after going through his eighth PEO interview like Bill Murray in "Groundhog Day," Mois had heard enough. He sought out Sgt. Mike Ratliff, his boss both in the homicide unit and on the task force. "It was a mirror of the last seven interviews I've done," Mois said. "There's nothing there." They agreed it was time to move on.

A number of task force investigators were currently going through the reams of pathology department personnel files that had been culled from Creighton. The records had been sorted into binders, each bearing the name of a current or former employee, and were now set out on shelves in the task force room. I'll see where we stand and get you one of those binders, Ratliff told Mois.

A half hour later, Ratliff walked up to Mois' desk and handed him a black binder containing the records of a former Creighton medical resident — a book that over the next 48 hours would dramatically alter the course of this investigation.

Mois for the first time read the name on the spine: Dr. Anthony J. Garcia.

CHAPTER 12: MORE THAN A NAME

Means, motive and opportunity. It's Homicide 101, Derek Mois would later say, a mantra drilled into every detective's head.

Means, motive and opportunity together make up the three elements of a crime, and the three pillars of guilt that often must be proven in court to make for a successful criminal prosecution. Find someone who had the tools to commit the crime (means), a reason to commit it (motive), and who was there at the right time and place (opportunity), and you just might have your man.

With that in mind, Mois sat down with a mug of coffee and a pad of Post-It notes the afternoon of May 27 and started sifting page-by-page through the Creighton University personnel files of Dr. Anthony J. Garcia. In those dry pages, Mois was looking for anything out of the ordinary.

The first pages of the Anthony Garcia file were medical licensing documents that shed some light on his history. Garcia was a native of California and had received his medical degree in May 1999 from the University of Utah in Salt Lake City. Mois could see from his birth date that Garcia was now just a week shy of 40.

Dr. Garcia had come to Creighton as a medical resident, a freshly minted medical school grad who was seeking on-the-job training in his chosen medical specialty of pathology.

Mois also saw Garcia had started his pathology residency at Creighton in July of 2000, some 13 years earlier.

Mois quickly saw something else noteworthy about Garcia's time at Creighton: he'd been fired. The records showed he'd been booted out of the school in May 2001, just 11 months into the four-year program. In documents related to that firing, Mois also saw a name that kept coming up: Dr. Chhanda Bewtra.

As Mois read on, it soon became clear that Garcia and Bewtra were having a pretty serious conflict in the weeks leading up to the firing, the dispute spelled out in copied memos and emails. Given the Bewtra break-in just hours before the Brumbacks were slain, Mois' interest in this Dr. Garcia was on the rise. Mois was suddenly placing sticky notes highlighting his observations all over the file. "Every time I turned a page," Mois would later say, "I was learning something new I thought was relevant."

Then Mois flipped a page and saw something that shook him: Garcia's actual termination letter. It was dated May 22, 2001. And most striking were the two signatures at the bottom:

William J. Hunter, M.D., and Roger A. Brumback, M.D.

Fuck, Mois thought. This guy had motive to kill everybody. Hunter, Brumback and Bewtra. The detective's interest in Garcia suddenly was rising exponentially.

Mois became so struck by the possibilities Garcia presented that by mid-afternoon, he decided to have a department technician run the doctor's name through the "Triple I" — essentially a nationwide criminal arrest record database maintained by the FBI.

The search didn't show much of a criminal history for Garcia. The only rap on his sheet was a very recent DUI in suburban Chicago. That arrest record listed Garcia at a Terre Haute,

Indiana, address. It also gave a physical description for the man: Ht: 5-8. Wt: 250. Skin: Olive.

Olive skin. Some of the witnesses in the Dundee case had used that exact word to describe the complexion of the mysterious man who had come and gone from the Hunter home in March 2008. Mois put a sticky note on that, too.

Mois was so engrossed with his reading of Garcia's file he ended up staying late into the evening. By the time the detective headed for home, this doctor who had been completely unknown to him hours earlier still had not risen to the level of suspect in his eyes.

But if anyone had asked Mois at the moment, he would certainly have described Garcia as "a person of interest."

* * *

On May 28, Mois' second day with his nose in Garcia's Creighton files, the detective put in a call to the police department in Terre Haute. He asked a detective there for any records they had for Garcia: contacts with police, auto registrations, gun licenses. Terre Haute detective Darren Long was very open to helping out, the next day emailing Mois a report of what he'd found.

Included in the May 29 multi-page document was an image of Garcia's Indiana driver's license. For the first time Mois got a look at Garcia, a meaty-faced man who indeed had olive skin.

Mois saw in the records previous addresses for Garcia, including Omaha; Chicago; Walnut, California; and Shreveport, Louisiana. This doctor had been around. Looking at Garcia's vehicle records, Mois saw the doctor currently had both a black Mercedes SUV and a Ferrari registered to him. Then Mois flipped to page 11 of the report, and his heart skipped a beat.

From June 2007 through June 2009, the vehicle registered to Garcia at his address in Louisiana had been a Honda CRV.

Oh shit.

Mois wasted no time making his way back over to the department's database technician, the same person who had given him the report on Garcia's criminal history two days earlier. This time, he asked her to run the vehicle identification number for Garcia's old CRV. Mois wanted to learn more about this vehicle, particularly its color.

The result came back in an instant, and for Mois it jumped right off the screen.

COLOR: SIL.

At that moment, everything else in Mois' world completely fell away. The vehicle was silver. A silver Honda CRV — the exact description several witnesses had given for the car driven by the Dundee killer.

This sent Mois' mind racing, the thoughts flashing through his head like electricity. At long last, could this really be the guy?

Mois could also see in the report that the CRV was currently registered to a Frederick Joseph Garcia in California. It appeared a relative of Garcia still had the car.

Mois drew in a deep breath and pondered his next move. Then he got on his computer and found a website where he could peruse images of state license plates from years past. Looking through the Louisiana plate images, he took particular interest in the one that appeared on passenger vehicles in that state during 2008. That plate displayed a pelican silhouetted against a sunset of yellow and pink.

Mois printed off the image and carried it over to the desk of task force detective Doug Herout. Mois knew Herout, a longtime homicide detective, years earlier had extensively researched the plate on the SUV that the Dundee witnesses had observed. "Is this at all consistent with what the witnesses saw?" Mois asked.

"That looks pretty good," Herout replied. "Absolutely. That could be it." Just to be sure, Herout opened a drawer and pulled out his old reports. The witnesses indeed described the plate as prominently featuring pastel colors like peach or pink. The two detectives agreed this plate fit the description.

Mois also asked Herout about Garcia. Herout had been the prime interrogator of Bill Hunter the night his son was killed. "Has this guy ever come up?" Mois asked. Herout said Hunter never mentioned Garcia to him at all.

Mois started back for his desk, the significance of what he'd just found sinking into his soul. In the five years since Dundee, he and other detectives had been absolutely bedeviled by their inability to figure out who was behind the wheel of the silver Honda CRV. Now, for the first time, here was a person of interest who drove a vehicle of the same make and color as that 2008 mystery man. Mois knew this could well be the most significant break ever in Dundee.

Up to this point, Mois had been keeping Sgt. Ratliff apprised of his growing interest in Garcia. Now Mois felt Garcia had risen to another level entirely. We need to put this guy under a microscope, Mois told Ratliff. And to do that, Mois would need some help. He wanted Ryan Davis and Nick Herfordt, two task force members who were on Mois' regular detective team in homicide, to work with him on a deep dive into Garcia.

"I need Ryan and I need Nick," he told Ratliff. "And I need everyone to leave us the fuck alone."

Ratliff agreed. He could see Mois was potentially on to something big. The rest of the task force investigators would continue to follow their own paths. But from this point on, Mois, Herfordt and Davis would be laser-focused on just one man.

CHAPTER 13: TEAM GARCIA

Derek Mois told very few people about it. He didn't want anyone to think he was nuts. But twice in the five years since Dundee, Mois had awoken in his bedroom to see Tom Hunter standing right over him.

There was the 11-year-old, with his wiry frame, shock of brown hair and round eyeglasses. The vision was so vivid, so clear, it was Tom in the flesh. Mois even felt the boy's presence.

Both times it happened, Mois sat up with a start, a chill charging down his spine. In the dark, he composed himself. He tried to rationalize what he'd seen.

Mois didn't believe in ghosts. The afterlife or such spiritual matters held no meaning to him. In the end, he had to conclude it had all been just a dream, one conjured by subconscious regret over never solving the boy's murder.

Now years later, Mois felt he truly might be on the verge of finally securing justice for Tom and his family. If Dr. Anthony Garcia indeed had anything to do with the murders of Tom, Shirlee and the Brumbacks, Mois was committed to making sure he was called to account. The detective absolutely would not rest until he did.

Mois' drive at that moment could be well summed up by the lyrics of a song by the indie band Lord Huron that Mois would later post above his desk. From the moment Mois heard "The Yawning Grave," it seemed to him to speak directly to a homicide detective's relationship with the killer in his sights:

Oh you fool, there are rules, I am coming for you.

Darkness brings evil things, oh the reckoning begins.

With their new assignment, Mois and partners Davis and Herfordt now rarely showed up in the task force operations room. They instead took their work back to their regular desks, sitting elbow-to-elbow in the fourth-floor homicide section. Not only was Mois happy to be working back in these cramped but familiar quarters, he was quite comfortable with the guys he was working with.

Herfordt, five months shy of his 40th birthday, brought much to the newly formed Team Garcia. With silver-streaked hair and olive skin — his grandfather was Santee Sioux, rooted on the tribe's reservation in northeast Nebraska — Herfordt was a solid homicide investigator known for his love of food trucks and McRib sandwiches, offbeat sense of humor and ease around computers. In recent years, he'd become the department's foremost expert in the fast-emerging field of digital forensics — mining evidence from cell phones, computers and other electronic devices.

That role had come naturally to Herfordt, the son of an Omaha computer programmer. Back in 1997, amid looming fears of Y2K computer meltdowns, Herfordt had decided to follow his father into the field. After enrolling in an accelerated study program, he soon realized he knew more about computers than his instructor did. Herfordt dropped the class and landed a job with an Omaha firm. But after the 9/11 terrorist attacks, Herfordt felt a calling to do something more. He left the corporate world two years later and got on with the Omaha police.

Herfordt was no gung-ho cop, and he didn't consider himself one. Unlike many of his brothers in blue, he abhorred guns and didn't even like carrying one. He just saw law enforcement as a profession that fit his skills and let him do some good.

Herfordt soon after became a detective and over time took on the role as the bureau's unofficial go-to guy on all things relating to computers or technology. They'd hand him a Rubik's Cube of a problem and he'd hand it back with all the colors matched up.

That's why when the department for the first time decided to assign a detective to work in digital forensics, Herfordt was an obvious candidate. For the past two years, Herfordt had been splitting his time between investigating murders and cyber-sleuthing for clues on seized cell phones and computers. Herfordt embraced this new role, later taking on the Twitter handle "Nerd Cop."

The nickname was typical of Herfordt's fun-loving ways. Around homicide, he was the guy who kept everyone loose with his crackpot humor and practical jokes. If you arrived at work and found a Hulk Hogan action figure or a cryptic note set out on your desk, you knew to go talk to Nick. Warner was his favorite target. With a straight face, Herfordt told his colleagues that he one day hoped to use his technical knowledge to become a Lex Luthor-like super villain after he retired.

As the Garcia team in the weeks ahead delved deeper into their target's background, Herfordt would lighten things up by initiating a game he called "Dr. Tony Trivia" — quizzing the team on obscure, often off-color details he'd pulled out of Garcia's past.

"Most of his stuff is so inappropriate," Mois would later say of Herfordt. "He's not stable."

But when it came time to play detective, Herfordt was dogged. And he was intent on learning everything he could about Garcia. Herfordt's oldest son was about the same age as Tom Hunter when he died. It was impossible for the detective not to think about what Tom went through, and the immense pain the crime brought to his parents. "I wanted the person who snuffed out his life caught," he'd later say.

Davis, Mois' other new right-hand man in the Garcia case, was a relative newcomer to homicide, having joined the unit just a year earlier. But this was a job the 34-year-old had been preparing for his whole life.

Trim with wavy red hair, Davis grew up in blue-collar, ethnic South Omaha, the kind of neighborhoods where lots of guys grow up to be either crooks or cops. Davis always wanted to be the latter. So he studied criminal justice in college, already with an eye toward becoming a homicide detective. During his first week in the police training academy, he was asked where he wanted to be in 10 years. "I want to be working homicide," he replied.

To Davis, the homicide unit seemed a magical place. He wanted to be in that room. And after eight years as a street cop and detective, he finally landed there in 2012.

Davis would have a distinct memory of one of his first days in the unit. Mois led him back to a meeting room and closed the door. Then he showed him the old files for the Dundee case. Mois walked him through the details, what they knew, what they didn't, what they might have done differently. Davis could tell Mois was haunted by the case.

In homicide, no one was more enthusiastic than this newcomer. Fueled by the cans of energy drink he downed each morning, he'd eagerly take on any task thrown his way. He absolutely lived for this job.

Davis also became known around the unit for the way he looked up to the Mois. Even when Davis was working robbery, he used to come over to the homicide section to pick Mois' brain.

They did have much in common. Davis shared Mois' deliberate investigative approach. Like Mois, he put all he had into his cases. And he even had his own impressive collection of tattoos inked down both arms. There was a reason some Omaha cops dubbed Davis "Mini Mois." Davis always took it as a compliment.

As Davis joined the task force, the topic of one of Davis' college criminal justice research papers suddenly seemed awfully relevant: serial murder. From 1893 Chicago World's Fair stalker H.H. Holmes to modern-day terrors like Ted Bundy or Jeffrey Dahmer, Davis over time became a virtual encyclopedia of America's serial killers. He knew all their names and twisted ways.

Now Davis had this unique opportunity to track a serial killer of his own. He and Herfordt talked about it over lunch one day shortly after they'd been named to the task force. "Can you believe we're investigating a serial killer?" Herfordt said.

The new Garcia team sat down together for the first time on May 30, the day after Mois discovered Garcia's silver CRV. Their work at that point was completely hush-hush, even within the task force, known only to them and Ratliff. They felt getting too many people involved now risked having their probe run off the rails, with a million opinions of where to go next. They felt they knew what needed to be done.

Mois briefed Herfordt and Davis on what he'd found so far. They could see they still had lots to learn. Just who is Anthony Garcia? Understanding his life history and what made him tick would be crucial to establishing whether he indeed had true motive to harm Drs. Hunter and Brumback.

At this point, the detectives had only the barest outline of the man's life, gleaned from the Creighton records. But as the Garcia investigators over the coming six weeks reviewed hundreds of additional pages of records from Creighton and other medical schools where Garcia had spent time, covertly peeked at the doctor's emails and perused his financial records, they would paint a fuller portrait of Garcia. A dominant theme for Garcia's troubled life would emerge.

They would see Garcia struggled mightily over the previous decade to get his medical career off the ground. And in most of his professional failures, Garcia's firing from Creighton University often loomed large.

CHAPTER 14: THE TRIGGER

In July 2000, the heavy-set 27-year-old doctor arrived at Creighton University, a 122-year-old Jesuit institution that traced its history back to Omaha's frontier days. He went through two days of orientation. He was issued a beeper and a badge that gave him privileges at St. Joseph Hospital, the Catholic teaching hospital adjacent to the university's near-downtown campus. And he was issued two white lab coats embroidered with his name: Anthony Garcia M.D.

Dr. Garcia was one of three first-year residents hired for the new academic year in Creighton's pathology department. If all went well, four years later, he'd complete his training in this medical specialty, pass his national exam and become a board certified pathologist — his ticket to a lucrative medical career.

Early on, Garcia sent photos home to his proud parents, one of him standing in his bleached white coat, another of him peering into a microscope. "Here are some more pictures of me at work," he wrote.

It appears the budding pathologist's studies at the school got off to a decent start. Garcia received an outstanding review during his introductory monthly rotation. The Creighton faculty member overseeing the young doctor called him diligent and hard-working, glowingly concluding that he "has made the transition from 'clinician' to 'pathologist.'"

The records showed Garcia did particularly well in another early rotation — hematology, the study of blood.

But as the Omaha detectives would learn years later, it didn't take long for Creighton colleagues to begin seeing troubling signs in this new doctor.

During conferences with supervising Creighton faculty, Garcia would cut up like a middle-schooler, making noises and rudely carrying on. He listened to no one. When Dr. Chhanda Bewtra one day asked the jerky resident to get out of the conference room, he refused. "I don't feel like it," he mocked. "I'll do what I want."

For someone who'd graduated from medical school, this was shockingly unprofessional behavior. On top of that, Garcia's work in the lab was found to be severely lacking.

The doctor showed a lack of basic medical knowledge and seemingly little interest in his chosen field. When it came time for Garcia's six-month review, a couple of his supervising physicians declined to even fill out evaluations, one later acknowledging he feared putting something so negative down in writing.

But Dr. Bewtra didn't hold anything back. She was always very frank and honest in her dealings with residents, focused on closing gaps in knowledge and performance. And she was quite blunt in her evaluations of Garcia. Her first official review of Garcia in the fall of 2000 was scathing, rating his attitude, knowledge and performance as simply unacceptable.

"Very passive-aggressive," she wrote. "Dr. Garcia showed marked lack of initiative and interest. He took no responsibility for his cases. His knowledge ... is very poor. When specifically asked to read up on certain topics and report back, he never did."

This whole Garcia mess ultimately landed on the desk of Bill Hunter. Dr. Hunter had just weeks earlier taken over as program director of the pathology residency program. He'd been asked to assume the post by Brumback, who himself had not long before arrived from Oklahoma as the pathology department's new chairman. As residency director, Hunter's job was to oversee the faculty evaluations of the residents' progress and serve as a mentor.

Hunter knew little about Garcia, the resident having been accepted into the department under the previous administration. But as Hunter looked into the background of this problem student, he began to wonder how Garcia had gotten into Creighton at all.

Hunter could see from Garcia's file that while he graduated from the University of Utah's medical school in 1999, it had taken him five years instead of the normal four. He three times failed a test on the basic science underpinnings of medicine, an exam medical students must pass before they can continue on to their third year. And the reviews of his critical internal medicine rotation were damning.

Hunter would years later learn of another black mark on Garcia's resume, one that was unknown to him back in 2001. The Creighton residency was not even Garcia's first. He had previously been drummed out of a family practice residency in Albany, New York.

The reports out of Bassett St. Elizabeth Medical Center in 1999 suggest Garcia was not only a bad doctor, but a dangerous one. He several times prescribed inappropriate medications for patients, once ordering a sedative for a patient whose chart said in big red letters DO NOT SEDATE. He took an afternoon nap while overseeing maternity patients who were in active labor. He lied about how completely he'd examined a patient.

Garcia always blamed others for his mistakes. Words that Bassett faculty members used to describe him would have certainly had a familiar ring to those who met him later at Creighton: lack of basic knowledge; lazy, lax and uninterested; surly and unreceptive to correction; arrogant and inappropriate behavior around staff and patients. "At the present time, you appear headed for disaster," the residency director wrote to him.

There also would be indications in the New York records that doctors there felt Garcia had some type of documentable personality disorder. The residency director put him on suspension and ordered him into counseling, suggesting he would need neuropsychological testing and therapy for any possible "underlying medical disorders."

It's unclear whether he underwent that evaluation. But his antisocial personality is what finally got Garcia bounced out eight months into the residency. His ouster followed an incident in which he yelled at a radiology technician.

"Don't give me your shit!" he screamed in front of a 12-year-old patient when the technician asked why he wasn't responding to her. Garcia chose to resign rather than face a disciplinary hearing on the incident.

Alarming as the New York revelations sound, Creighton didn't know anything about them. Dr. Garcia failed to disclose the previous residency in his application to the school. Still, such a one-year time gap in a resume always suggests possible problems. Hunter believed it was a red flag the previous administration should have caught and explored more deeply.

Looking back, Garcia's past indeed does beg the question: Exactly how did he get into Creighton? "That's what I keep asking," Hunter would lament in an interview years later.

Not only were his credentials poor, Creighton's typical interview process for new residents — in which several faculty members and current residents have the chance to meet with the job candidate — had not been followed in his hiring.

Hunter would later have his speculations as to what happened. As a small medical school far from the coasts, Creighton at times had difficulty attracting top-flight American medical school grads. In those years, it would often instead fill some residency openings by falling back on graduates of foreign medical schools.

Such international med school grads were most often solid doctors but at times came with their own challenges, including language barriers. And at the time Garcia was accepted at Creighton, the school's pathology program was heavily populated by such foreign residents. Hunter surmised the previous department chair decided to fish at the bottom of the domestic candidate pool rather than accept yet another foreign resident. But it was a horrible decision. Hunter wasn't the only one in the department who would find it hard to believe Garcia was ever hired by Creighton.

Still, regardless of how Garcia had landed at the school, Hunter in 2001 also knew that Garcia had now become Creighton's problem. And Hunter was committed to doing what he could to help the resident succeed.

Hunter by his nature was a humble, caring and good-natured man who tended to see the good in people. In the medical school, he was known as a student-centered educator who advocated for his students. He was always willing to go the extra mile for them. For that reason, he was beloved among students and had won several teaching awards.

When it came to weak or struggling residents like Garcia, Hunter's philosophy was to work patiently with them during their first year and give them time to correct any deficiencies. He found they usually took their issues to heart and eventually got up to speed. If serious problems persisted into the subsequent years of the four-year residency, that's when Hunter felt it was time to draw the line.

One of the few people who didn't care for Hunter's ways was his boss. Brumback, the department chair, told Hunter he didn't think he was strict enough with residents. It would become a regular source of conflict between them. Hunter simply disagreed with Brumback's more stern approach.

True to his nature, Hunter sat down with Garcia in January 2001. He kindly noted all the problems reported by Bewtra and others. He gently prodded the young doctor, suggesting Garcia show more enthusiasm for his work.

Hunter wasn't impressed with the resident's response. Garcia seemed paranoid, believing his evaluators were out to get him. This guy has a real chip on his shoulder, Hunter thought.

From there, Garcia's problems only escalated. As Bewtra gave Garcia another bad review during a February conference, Garcia launched into a belligerent tirade, calling her names. Bewtra argued that Garcia should be immediately put on probation for possible termination. "Bill, how many more documentations do you need?" she asked Hunter in a note.

Garcia claimed Bewtra was the one in the wrong, saying she had many times "humiliated, degraded and insulted me." He sent a letter to Creighton's chief resident threatening to file a lawsuit. "Bewtra hounds you by saying, 'you should know this' and 'why don't you know this,'" he wrote in another email to Creighton officials. "She uses her position to verbally abuse residents she works with."

Despite Garcia's protestations, Hunter trusted Bewtra's reviews. He knew her to be a tough but fair and level-headed educator. And Hunter had also recently observed firsthand an incident in which Garcia was contentious, defensive and disrespectful after another faculty evaluator who oversaw a Garcia autopsy pointed out the resident's faulty technique and misdiagnosis.

"This guy needs an attitude adjustment," the colleague told Hunter afterwards. Hunter agreed. He, too, now believed Garcia had some type of personality disorder.

Then just days later, Garcia made an error that proved a major embarrassment to Creighton. After an autopsy, he'd left the body of a woman face down overnight, disfiguring her face. The outraged funeral home director registered a complaint with the school.

Brumback was furious. He called Garcia into his office and read him the riot act, accusing him of mutilating the body. Amazingly, Garcia didn't seem to understand why they were making such a big deal out of this.

Hunter was now in agreement with Brumback and Bewtra. He wanted Garcia gone. But Hunter still wasn't ready to kick Garcia to the curb.

For one, it was legally hard to fire a resident. They practically had to murder someone before you could boot them out mid-year. Second, he believed if Garcia could make it through the year, a change of scenery might do him some good. He had previously seen residents flourish in such circumstances.

But the biggest driver in Hunter's thinking was this: In medical circles, it was a huge black mark to be dismissed from a residency program. For a doctor, it could well be a career killer.

Instead, Hunter's hope was that Garcia could get through the rest of the academic year and walk away with a certificate for a full year of training. He could then seek a medical future elsewhere. It was the "humane thing to do," Hunter thought.

So as Hunter and Garcia walked out of Brumback's office after the autopsy incident, Hunter told him the school would probably not be renewing his contract for the second year. He needed to be looking for another job. Hunter cautioned him to keep his nose clean until the school year ended in June. "You're digging your own grave here," he told him.

Garcia seemed at first to take the decision as an affront. Hunter wasn't sure how he would respond. "I hope he takes our offer to go quietly, otherwise he'll have trouble finding another position," Hunter wrote soon after to a colleague.

Despite Garcia's initial reaction, it seems the non-renewal notice did ultimately get his attention. Because the doctor soon after expressed a desire to stay at Creighton and resolve his problems. "I will change to be the resident the faculty wants," he pledged in writing to Hunter.

Hunter sat down with the young doctor and again counseled him, urging him to work with his teachers. He also asked him to apologize directly to Dr. Bewtra. Hunter put the terms down in writing, and Garcia agreed to them. "I am sorry if any of my words have insulted you, a teacher whose efforts shape the future minds of pathologists," Garcia awkwardly wrote to Bewtra in mid-March.

For the next two months, Garcia's performance did somewhat improve. In mid-May, the Creighton doctor overseeing his latest rotation gave an encouraging review. Garcia had interacted well with others and gave well-received presentations. It seemed to Hunter that Garcia might be able to squeak through after all.

But just two days later came an incident that finally forced even Hunter's hand.

While the chief resident was in the midst of taking a high-stakes national exam that would determine whether he would be licensed to practice medicine, someone called his wife and said he was urgently needed at Creighton. If he didn't report right away, the caller claimed, he'd be fired.

Creighton officials saw the incident as, at the very least, harassment, and at worst, a deliberate effort to sabotage the resident's exam. And they quickly determined Garcia was behind it. He and another resident had been overheard conspiring over the deed in Creighton's "gross room," the aptly named lab where pathologists dissect human tissue samples.

That was it. Hunter the next day prepared a lengthy memo documenting Garcia's litany of failures. University attorneys got involved. Then on May 22, the doctor was summoned to Brumback's office. Hunter read aloud Garcia's official letter of dismissal.

Garcia denied any knowledge of the harassment incident, even after he was confronted with the fact he'd been overheard masterminding the plot.

Hunter gave Garcia a choice: He could immediately resign, or he would be fired. Garcia chose to be fired, doing so to enable him to appeal the decision to the dean of the medical school. A school security guard was there to escort Garcia out, but it was unnecessary. Garcia was docile and passive as he left the pathology department for the last time.

Both Hunter and Brumback subsequently testified during a hearing on Garcia's appeal, which the dean denied. His firing became official on July 12, 2001. While a number of pathology residents in the past had failed to have their contracts renewed, or had been convinced to leave voluntarily, Garcia was the first Hunter could ever recall who was outright fired.

Garcia contemplated suing Creighton. But, in the end he left quietly, with no further fuss. Then, amazingly — thanks in large part to Hunter — Garcia actually landed on his feet.

Just two months after his Creighton dismissal, Garcia was accepted into another pathology residency, at the University of Illinois College of Medicine in Chicago. The ever-gracious Hunter had written a generic letter of recommendation for

Garcia and then vouched for him to his counterpart at the school. Hunter expressed his belief — seemingly hoping beyond all hope — that Garcia could still succeed. "I was probably over-optimistic," Hunter would say years later of his final effort to help Garcia. "But I thought maybe in another environment, he'd be OK."

Garcia was also helped by the fact the Chicago school had a pathology opening as the academic year was starting and a quota to fill. But if Hunter or anyone was optimistic about Garcia's third residency, it wouldn't be borne out. The administrator who hired Garcia would later say it was the stupidest decision he ever made. Garcia wouldn't make it through two years in Chicago.

If Garcia suffered from some kind of personality disorder at Creighton, it appears in Chicago he fell into a deeper mental health abyss. He was plagued by migraines, depression and poor health that caused him to take long leaves of absence. Records would later show he racked up $80,000 in medical bills, many of them to neurologists and psychiatrists.

In failure, in 2003 Garcia drifted back home to his parents in Walnut, California, a well-off suburb in Los Angeles' inland valley. Under a mountain of medical debt, he filed for bankruptcy in 2005. According to a Garcia email the Omaha detectives obtained, Garcia worked at home fixing cars and debated whether he wanted to try to continue in medicine.

But again, Garcia somehow was able to resurrect his medical career from the scrap heap. In 2007, he was accepted into a psychiatry residency at Louisiana State University Health Sciences Center in Shreveport.

There had been no mention of LSU in the Creighton records Mois had originally viewed. But on June 12, Herfordt received records he had requested from Bassett. In those files was a recent application by Garcia for a medical license in Kentucky that listed the LSU residency.

Herfordt requested the LSU records, too. When those records came in days later, the detectives could see the LSU residency proved no more successful than Garcia's previous three. And significantly, they also saw that his Creighton firing — and Garcia's efforts to conceal it — were at the center of his undoing.

Garcia received a temporary license to practice medicine in Louisiana while the state medical board reviewed his credentials. As was typical in such reviews, the board contacted previous schools to verify the training Garcia listed on his application. They reached out to Bill Hunter at Creighton.

In his job as residency director, Hunter routinely handled hundreds of such verification requests each year, coming from medical boards, other medical schools, hospitals and other health care employers. Given Garcia's problems at Creighton, though, verifications in his case were less-than-routine. Procedure called for Hunter to run them first by the school's legal department.

Some verification requests merely ask for dates of training. Others ask specific questions about program completion and performance. The request in this case called for some level of detail. Hunter told Louisiana the resident had been fired before completing his first year of training.

For the licensing board, Hunter's response was particularly notable because it didn't square with Garcia's license application. In that document, Garcia had suggested he did finish a full year at Creighton. In addition, Garcia had falsely answered "no" on part of the application that asked whether he'd ever been the subject of a disciplinary action.

Citing the falsehoods and omissions, the state medical board in February of 2008 notified LSU officials of its intention to deny Garcia a license. Garcia could still continue his training at LSU under his temporary license, but LSU officials realized the doctor had likely lied on his original application to them, too.

Days later, Hunter's LSU counterpart gave him a call. Hunter verified that Garcia had indeed been fired by Creighton in 2001, also during that interview terming him a "weak resident."

On Feb. 26, 2008, LSU officials summoned Garcia into the office. They then dismissed him, citing his Creighton omissions.

Garcia argued he'd been wronged by Creighton's "racist" program. He would have sued Creighton if he'd had the money, he said that day. LSU officials told him he could appeal his termination. He demurred. "I'll move on," he said. He was escorted off the premises.

But this time, as events in Omaha would soon prove, he did not go quietly.

Indeed, as Mois, Herfordt and Davis worked at their desks in Omaha piecing together Garcia's life story, the details of Garcia's LSU firing proved a major revelation. When Herfordt received the package of records from LSU, he saw the firing date and quickly realized its significance: Feb. 26 was just 16 days before the murders of Tom Hunter and Shirlee Sherman.

Now it all made sense. It wasn't as if Garcia had stewed for seven years over his Creighton firing before acting on it. There had been a much more immediate trigger for the killings.

Herfordt would later say it was never confirmed in his subsequent interviews with LSU officials that they had specifically told Garcia when they dismissed him about their phone conversation with Hunter. But regardless, it would have been clear to Garcia that his Creighton firing was the reason he was being terminated. For the detectives, this was a huge development, creating a rock solid, proximate motive for the Dundee slayings.

At that point, the detectives followed Garcia's paper trail from LSU back to Chicago, where he soon after moved. It wasn't clear to the detectives, but it seemed likely he returned to Illinois because it was the only state to grant Garcia a medical license. Though obtained for his Chicago residency seven years earlier, it was still valid.

Back in the Windy City, the detectives could see from Garcia's email records that by 2009 he'd been able to land work with a couple of medical clinics, including one that sent doctors on house calls to elderly Medicare patients. It wasn't lucrative work for a doctor, but it was a paycheck.

Then by 2010, Garcia landed another job with a contractor that was providing health care for inmates at the federal prison in Terre Haute. The prison in that Indiana city where Garcia soon after relocated is best known for the special confinement unit in which federal prisoners who've been sentenced to death are held. Oklahoma City bomber Timothy McVeigh was executed within the prison's walls in 2001.

As he had at LSU, Garcia practiced in Indiana on a temporary license. But then when Garcia subsequently sought a permanent license from the state of Indiana, his past came back to haunt him again.

The Indiana medical licensing board in 2012 contacted Creighton to verify Garcia's training. This time, Roger Brumback gave the response, having permanently taken over the department's verification duties from Hunter in the wake of his son's 2008 murder.

Brumback told Indiana about Garcia's firing. "Garcia was involved in an incident that the program felt was unprofessional behavior toward a fellow resident," Brumback wrote to the medical board in September 2012.

Based at least in part on this information, the Indiana licensing board denied Garcia a license in December 2012.

There would be no indication that Garcia specifically knew that Brumback had played a direct role in his Indiana license denial. But Mois later said it's believed he did receive some degree of information on why the license was denied, and his Creighton failure again clearly played a significant role. Within five months of the license denial, Brumback was dead.

For Team Garcia, the additional medical records uncovered in recent weeks had been a goldmine. It seemed they'd revealed concrete motive for both of the doctor's deadly house calls in Omaha: a pathological drive for revenge against the pathology doctors at Creighton who he blamed for his failures.

Buried in the all the medical records was one other tidbit that, while not particularly significant to the case the detectives were building, was at least of morbid interest.

During her hold-nothing-back review of Garcia's work in the lab and classroom in late 2000, Chhanda Bewtra had actually given Garcia high marks in one area. She noted he showed skill in cutting the tissue samples that pathologists analyze in the lab.

In other words, he was good with a knife.

CHAPTER 15: THE BIG BREAK

Traveling with an FBI agent, detective Scott Warner checked in at Omaha's airport on June 14. He was set to fly off to Washington state for what was still seen as one of the most critical moments of the Omaha task force investigation — an interview with the Russian.

Almost from the moment the Brumbacks' bodies were discovered, Warner had been preparing for this interview. Despite five years of serious vetting since the 2008 Dundee murders, the former Creighton pathology resident was still seen at the start as the best suspect the task force had. The plan was for Warner to fly west and surprise the Russian at the cabin in the woods of northern Washington where he now lived, just miles from the Canadian border.

Just before Warner and the agent boarded their plane, Warner got on the phone with Mois. While the two longtime homicide partners had pursued their separate tracks during the task force investigation, they stayed in regular contact. Mois had kept Warner in the loop on what he was learning about Garcia, counting on Warner's advice during those "what's next?" and "what am I missing?" moments. Now Mois razzed his friend about flying cross country on the taxpayers' dime.

"You're out there chasing ghosts, and I'm here finding the real guy," Mois teased.

Mois by now was indeed convinced his team was on to the right guy. Each new discovery about Garcia was only fueling Mois' fire all the more. He had barely taken a day off since the moment he picked up that Garcia binder. But there was still so much work to do.

Clearly Mois, Herfordt and Davis were finding Garcia had truckloads of motive to kill Hunter and Brumback. But the detectives needed to now establish that Garcia was actually in Omaha at the time of the killings. And that was proving frustrating and elusive.

The rise of the digital age has given investigators a couple of critical tools to prove where a person was at any given time in the past: cell phone calls and credit card transactions. Almost everyone carries a cell phone and makes purchases with plastic. Find out where and when a person uses them and you can pinpoint just where they were at a given date and time.

The detectives had quickly determined that the cell phone number that showed up in some of Garcia's Creighton files was still an active one. Davis wrote up a search warrant for those phone records. At the same time, Mois went after Garcia's credit cards.

A run of Garcia's name through a credit rating agency showed he in recent years had almost too many credit cards to count. Mois was soon up to his neck in search warrants, having to seek records from 20 different banks.

Mois could see this was going to take some time. In fact, the effort dragged on for weeks. But finally at 9:15 a.m. on June 25 — nearly a month into their focus on Garcia — an email landed in Mois' inbox.

It was from AT&T, a file containing the call log for Garcia's cell phone.

Mois downloaded the records to a computer disc and handed it to Herfordt, who was most familiar with such records. Herfordt sat down at his computer. With Mois standing over his shoulder, and Davis right behind him, they started sifting through the data.

The records didn't go back far enough in time to cover the Dundee killings. But Herfordt soon found that on Mother's Day 2013, there was a single phone call on Garcia's log: an incoming call at 5:18 p.m. that went unanswered, going to voicemail. The detectives saw the time of the call could well fit into their working timeline for the Brumback killings, coming less than two hours after the gunshots heard by the neighbors.

Next to that call in the log were two multi-digit numbers. Herfordt knew they represented latitude and longitude lines, their intersection point being the location of the cell phone tower that had routed the call to Garcia's phone. It was, in effect, a digital fingerprint that Garcia's iPhone had left behind that day.

Herfordt noted the coordinates: 41.49047 latitude, -95.0527 longitude. And then he anxiously typed the numbers into Google maps.

The detectives peered at the screen with breathless anticipation as Herfordt hit send. This was a real moment of truth. It was time to get beyond gut feelings and hunches. If the right result came up, they'd have irrefutable evidence that Garcia had been in Omaha that day. Conversely, if the map showed he was at home in Terre Haute, they'd be depressingly back to square one.

On the screen, a map came up. At first, they weren't familiar with any landmarks that popped up. Herfordt zoomed out for a wider view and found the cell tower was in ... remote, mountainous northern China, near the Mongolian border. What?!

Oh no, wait, Herfordt said. He right away realized that in his haste, he'd dropped the negative sign before the longitude number, sending the detectives to the wrong hemisphere of the globe. Herfordt corrected it, hit send again, and they all again peered intently into the screen.

Bingo.

On the new map that came up, the detectives immediately saw names and places they recognized. There was Interstate 80, the buzzing freeway linking Omaha to both coasts. There were several familiar towns, little ones just miles across the Missouri River in neighboring Iowa.

The cell phone tower that had routed that call to Garcia's phone May 12 was located along I-80 near Atlantic, Iowa, just an hour east of Omaha.

"That's it," Davis said excitedly. "We got him." The detective team high-fived and bro-hugged in celebration, jubilant in the moment. "When western Iowa popped up on the screen," Herfordt would later say, "it was like getting injected with 1.21 gigawatts of adrenaline."

For Mois, this was the breakthrough he'd been chasing for more than five years. Not only did Garcia have clear motive to kill the Brumbacks, but these phone records also showed he had the opportunity to do so. And given his physical description, the car he was driving in 2008 and the timing of the LSU firing, he was the strongest suspect Omaha police had ever identified in the 2008 Dundee homicides.

In 29 days, Garcia had gone from being just a name on a binder to now being the prime suspect in the deaths of Roger and Mary Brumback, Tom Hunter and Shirlee Sherman. There was now no doubt. They had their man, even if at the moment they likely couldn't prove that in a court of law.

"At that point, he had moved from a person of interest to a suspect," Mois later recalled. "I remember thinking, 'This is good. But we still have a long ways to go.'"

CHAPTER 16: 'DO WE HAVE ENOUGH?'

Behind the covered-over windows of the sixth-floor task force operations room, the air buzzed as Team Garcia assembled with task force commanders, Omaha Police Chief Todd Schmaderer and Brenda Beadle, the chief deputy in the Douglas County Attorney's Office.

It was now July 12, six weeks after Mois, Herfordt and Davis had started on the trail of Anthony Garcia, and three weeks since they got the cell tower hit. It was time for prosecutors to decide whether there was enough evidence to seek a warrant for Garcia's arrest. And it was up to Mois, Herfordt and Davis to make the sale.

This wasn't just an academic exercise. If the task force was going to arrest Garcia, its leaders wanted to be sure they had enough evidence to prove his guilt in court. At the same time, they all felt the clock was ticking. There remained very real concern that Garcia could at any time strike again. As they pondered what to do, lives could very well be hanging in the balance.

Mois, Davis and Herfordt had prepared a PowerPoint presentation detailing the evidence they'd gathered, ready to walk through it all. Included in those slides were some noteworthy new developments — information that in Mois' mind had really solidified the case for arresting Garcia.

Significantly, the detectives could now tie Garcia to the very model of gun that killed Roger Brumback. And they also knew much more about Garcia's whereabouts on that deadly Mother's Day in Omaha, able to place him in close proximity to the Brumback home just before the killings.

The new breakthroughs had started with Garcia's cell phone records, the same ones detectives had used to prove he was in neighboring Iowa on Mother's Day. The day after the discovery of the tell-tale Iowa call, Herfordt continued to work the records. He next wanted to see exactly who Garcia had been talking to on his phone, which might reveal more incriminating evidence. Going down the call log, Herfordt looked up each phone number for both incoming and outgoing calls in a reverse phone directory.

Herfordt first learned that the unanswered call placing Garcia across the river in Iowa had actually come from his parents in California, perhaps intended to be a Mother's Day conversation between mother and son. Among the other calls Herfordt discovered was one Garcia had placed to an outdoor outfitting store in Terre Haute called Gander Mountain.

Herfordt had never heard of Gander Mountain. While it was the largest chain of outdoor specialty stores in the country, it had no outlets within 250 miles of Omaha. Mois, though, an avid hunter and wilderness backpacker, was familiar with Gander Mountain. And he knew something else: Gander Mountain sold guns.

The detectives now wondered whether Garcia could have bought a gun from Gander Mountain. And they were looking for one gun model in particular. Thanks to the Omaha police department's resident gun guru, they already knew the exact make of gun that killed Roger Brumback.

Right after finishing the crime scene investigation at the Brumback home weeks before, Mois had gone to meet with Dan Bredow of the Omaha Police Department crime lab. Mois dropped on Bredow's desk all the gun parts collected from the floor of Brumback's home: the small broken-off, U-shaped piece of the frame, the rod and spring and the ammunition clip. He also presented Bredow the shell casing found in the doorway and a bullet slug found on the kitchen floor. "Can you tell me what kind of gun these came from?" Mois asked.

Mois knew from experience that if you ever wanted to know anything about a gun — and wanted to take that information to the bank — you go talk to Dan Bredow. The Omaha crime lab technician possessed an encyclopedic knowledge of firearms, from their history, manufacture, function and capabilities, right down to the damage they do when fired into human flesh and bone.

As usual, Bredow did not disappoint. He examined the parts, the rifling on the slug and the contact marks on the casing. And the very next day, he got back to Mois. This isn't official because I haven't finished my report yet, Bredow told Mois in an email. "But you're looking for an SD9."

Mois was quite familiar with the gun Bredow referred to: a Smith & Wesson SD9VE semi-automatic pistol. It was a 9-millimeter handgun with a distinctive two-tone finish, featuring a stainless steel slide, a textured grip and 16- to 17-round clip. Find someone with an SD9, Mois now knew, and you have a person with the means to kill Roger Brumback.

So weeks after that finding, Team Garcia was now seeing Gander Mountain in these phone records. They decided to play a hunch. Ryan Davis asked the Indiana state police to serve a search warrant at the store for records of any gun purchases by Garcia.

The next day, June 28, the results came back, and it was another bull's-eye shot. On March 8, 2013 — two months before the Brumback killings — Anthony Garcia went to Gander Mountain and bought an SD9.

This was another huge finding. With the SD9, it seemed the detectives had potentially locked down means, motive and opportunity for Garcia to commit the Brumback murders.

With all that Mois and the task force now had in hand, some command officers were getting antsy, feeling it was time to swoop in. Chief Schmaderer himself had been closely following the case, coming down to the detective bureau himself one day to see Mois.

Days earlier, Schmaderer had been deflated when he'd been informed Warner had come back from his interview with the Russian unconvinced he was the killer. The prime suspect was now off the list. What do we have to go on now? That's when Schmaderer then was first briefed on what Mois, Herfordt and Davis had been up to. Sitting in Davis' chair right next to Mois, the chief then asked for a horse's mouth update on this new suspect.

Schmaderer remained concerned that Garcia could kill again. In fact, the detectives had other records showing Garcia had bought another gun recently, likely a replacement for his broken SD9. It suggested he might have more deadly plans. As soon as the detectives were ready, Schmaderer wanted Garcia taken off the street.

Mois, too, saw Garcia's gun purchase as an ominous sign. But he was among those still questioning whether they had enough evidence for the takedown. Mois also knew the detectives still had a significant card to play: Garcia's credit cards.

Those records in recent weeks had been coming in at a glacial pace. The detectives had requested records going all the way back to 2007, just prior to the Dundee killings. It was a lot of work for both the banks and the detectives, ultimately producing enough paperwork to fill two file boxes. Yet up to that point, the reams of records produced had been of limited value.

One of the banks Mois had not heard back from was Alabama-based Regions Bank. Feeling the urgency to act, Mois called Regions in late June for an update. He was told it would still take some time. Mois was now desperate.

"Can you get me a limited response?" he asked. If he narrowed the records request to only the past few months, could they expedite it? Regions agreed. And just over a week later, on July 9, those records came in.

Eyeballing the Regions statements, the Garcia team quickly found a reference to Omaha, Nebraska. Garcia had made a $7.69 charge at an Omaha business listed in the records as "Wingman."

Around the same time there was another transaction showing Garcia had spent $22.59 at a Casey's General Store convenience store. That record didn't say where the store was located, but Casey's had locations in and around Omaha.

Both purchases were dated May 14, two days after the Brumback killings. But Mois knew May 14 was just the date the transactions were posted by Regions. He'd need to go to the businesses themselves to document when the actual purchases had taken place. Mois tasked Davis to go chase down the Casey's purchase while he went after Wingman.

Mois had never heard of Wingman. But he soon figured out it was the corporate name for the Omaha franchises of a national chicken wing restaurant chain called Wingstop. Soon after, Mois was meeting the restaurants' owner at his home, where he maintained his business office. It probably took Bob Morrison only a few minutes to dig up the sales receipt, but as Mois stood there, it seemed an eternity.

Morrison finally handed the receipt to Mois.

It showed Garcia had stopped in at Morrison's 72nd and Pacific location. The time and date of the purchase were also printed right at the top of the receipt: 2:26 p.m. on May 12 — Mother's Day.

As with the phone records, this time fit perfectly with the detectives' working time line for that day. The wing purchase came just nine minutes after the intrusion alarm at Bewtra's. What's more, her home was just over a mile from Wingstop. When the detectives drove the route, it took just 2 minutes, 25 seconds to get there.

The restaurant was also just minutes away from the Brumback house. In fact, right about the time Garcia would have been sitting there eating his wings, the Brumbacks were wrapping up their Mother's Day chat with their daughter. With this receipt, Garcia's opportunity to kill the Brumbacks had now moved from Atlantic, Iowa, right into the heart of Omaha, just minutes from the Brumback home.

Davis likewise hit a home run on the Casey's purchase. Garcia had stopped at a Casey's in Council Bluffs, Iowa, right across the Missouri River from Omaha, at 12:38 p.m. on Mother's Day. And better yet, the store had surveillance video of the transaction.

In this day and age, it was common for businesses and even homeowners to employ security cameras, and they'd become an important crime-fighting tool. Such cameras stand as silent, perpetual witnesses to all going on around them. Whenever investigating a crime, detectives were always on the lookout for any cameras in the area that may have caught something.

The Casey's video, obtained by Davis the next day, captured Garcia at virtually every moment during his stop at the convenience store. One outside camera showed the arrival of Garcia's black Mercedes SUV. The view of another camera caught him walking inside and then disappearing into a restroom. The same camera showed him emerge minutes later, grab a case of warm Bud Light — yes, he strangely drank warm beer — and take it up to the register. Finally, yet another camera showed him put the beer up on the counter and pay for it, this camera view offering a good look at Garcia's chubby mug.

It seemed to the detectives that this beer purchase represented the liquid courage Garcia needed to commit his crimes hours later. It wasn't lost on Mois that the mystery man seen outside the Hunter home five years earlier had been seen to stumble. Perhaps alcohol had dulled Garcia's senses in both sets of slayings.

As Mois watched Garcia in the Casey's video, he knew this clip was almost bulletproof.

Garcia couldn't try to claim someone stole his card and used it that day. The man standing at the counter buying his Mother's Day beer across the river was clearly Garcia, in the flesh. The Terre Haute resident would have a hard time explaining away how he just happened to be there the day the man who fired him was murdered.

The video and wings receipt also helped alter Mois' thinking about arresting Garcia. We have enough, Mois thought. That decision, though, was not ultimately his to make. Douglas County Attorney Don Kleine and his chief deputy, Beadle, would decide.

Kleine and Beadle had long histories with both the Hunter and Brumback cases, having visited both crime scenes at the time of the killings. They often did so in high-profile crimes. While they could read every report and look over every photo, there was no substitute for scoping the scene with their own eyes.

The prosecutors had recently been receiving regular briefings on the task force's progress, including the growing interest in Garcia. Beadle had been in the task force room one day recently when Mois burst in with one of his team's new findings. At that moment, it had given her chills.

The prosecutors had also been feeling stress and anxiety over whether it was time to nab Garcia. The topic had already produced some tense discussions between Beadle and Kleine. Beadle, a veteran homicide litigator who had worked with Kleine for more than a decade, was the more edgy of the two. Kleine, the state's most seasoned prosecutor, had been urging caution.

The standard for conviction in court, of course, would be proof beyond a reasonable doubt. They didn't want to move too quickly with an arrest in a case they ultimately couldn't prove to a jury, Kleine argued. He thought it better to take the time to collect the evidence now rather than just hope they found more after an arrest. "Are we going to be able to develop more, or is this it?" he said. "Let's make sure we have our ducks in a row."

As it turned out, Kleine wasn't able to attend this key briefing in the task force room July 12. He was on the board of the National District Attorneys Association, which was holding its annual meeting in California. But Beadle went into the task force room with a deep understanding of where her boss stood. She knew what he wanted to see and hear.

Mois, Herfordt and Davis flashed their PowerPoint up on a screen, walking Beadle through their evidence slide by slide: Garcia's 2001 Creighton firing; the signature neck wounds of all four victims; Garcia's silver SUV with the pastel plate; the verification letters from Hunter and Brumback that seemed to trigger the double murders; the cell call near Omaha; Garcia's handgun; the wings receipt and the convenience store video.

Beadle was excited by what she was seeing. The detectives had unearthed some hard evidence, a firm foundation on which prosecutors could build a case. With a mix of both confidence and elation, Beadle made the call.

OK. Let's go.

With that decision, the recent breakneck pace of the Garcia investigators only accelerated. Mois was back in the office the next day, a Saturday. Again, there would be no rest for the detective.

Sitting down at his desk computer, Mois started batting out an affidavit for an arrest warrant. In a clipped, just-the-facts yet riveting narrative, he walked the as-yet unknown judge who'd be reading the document through Garcia's tale of failure, vengeance and blood.

"These affiant Officers further state that there is reasonable cause to believe the crime of First Degree murder, four counts, was committed and that said defendant committed said crime," Mois concluded in stiff, lawyerlike fashion.

As Mois finished and saved the document, the significance of the moment wasn't lost on him. It had been five long years since that warm March night in 2008 when he became the first detective to take in the awful scene in the Hunters' Dundee home. Now he and fellow Omaha cops were set to bring Tom and Shirlee's killer home to face justice.

CHAPTER 17: 'HE'S MOVING'

The commercial jet carrying the Omaha detectives broke through the clouds and touched down on the tarmac of Indianapolis International Airport. It was now Sunday, July 14, and the Omaha task force was ready to pounce.

The plan called for the detectives to pick up airport rental cars, drive to Terre Haute, set up in a hotel and coordinate with local law enforcement. And then in the predawn darkness early the next morning, they'd follow behind an Indiana State Police SWAT team that would kick down Garcia's door. Believing Garcia to be potentially armed and dangerous, the hope was to catch him in his sleep.

All seven Omaha officers who made the trip to Indiana had their assigned roles. Mois and Warner would immediately follow Garcia to jail and try to interview him. Davis and Herfordt would serve a search warrant on Garcia's home. Other detectives would fan out talking to neighbors, employers and anyone else who knew Garcia. At the same time, another team of task force officers was headed west. They would simultaneously hit Garcia's parents' home in California, serve a warrant and impound the silver CRV.

But the best laid plans of mice and men and, as it turns out, multiagency law enforcement task forces, often do go awry. Not long after the officers landed in Indianapolis, they were all thrown for a loop. Lt. Fidone checked her cell phone and saw it right away.

"Oh, my gosh," she said. "He's moving."

Since July 1, the task force had been secretly keeping an electronic eye on Garcia. Herfordt had gone to court for a search warrant authorizing the task force to "ping" Garcia's cell phone. Every half hour, Fidone and Sgt. Ratliff received an email from the phone company with the current GPS coordinates for the phone.

The last ping before the officers took off for Indy had shown Garcia at home in Terre Haute. They couldn't get new ping updates while in flight. But catching up in the Indianapolis airport terminal, Fidone could see Garcia had driven west across the border into Illinois. He appeared to still be moving south into downstate Illinois.

The task force members quickly gathered their equipment and headed out for the hour and a half drive to Terre Haute. Gathered later in a hotel room there, they could see Garcia was now two hours away in Salem, Illinois, a small town just off Interstate 57. He appeared to have stopped there, perhaps for the night.

Now they had to try to figure out what he was up to. The detectives knew from their surreptitious viewing of Garcia's emails that the doctor at times recently had been getting spot work doing contract wellness checks at various businesses. This move could be completely harmless. He might be out on such a job and before long would be back in Terre Haute.

But there were other possibilities, too. They had to wonder whether Garcia was in flight. Could he have somehow learned they were probing his background, or been tipped off by someone? Could he have figured out they were closing in on him?

They had another thought, too: Could he be on his way to kill again?

One of the reasons they'd started pinging Garcia's phone was concern the doctor at any time could return to Omaha on a new deadly mission. The task force leaders decided that if there was ever any indication Garcia was headed back to Omaha, they would arrest him immediately.

With the southern trajectory Garcia was currently on, it didn't look like he was bound for Omaha. But I-57 through Illinois was precisely the route one would take to get from Terre Haute to Shreveport. From their probing of Garcia's background, Mois, Davis and Herfordt knew there were still people in Shreveport who had a direct hand in Garcia's firing. "We had a strong concern this guy was a menace and could kill someone else," Herfordt would recall of the moment. "If he's on another vendetta, we need to stop him."

Taking all those things into consideration, the detectives plotted a new plan of action. And much of it came to revolve around a pair of Omaha FBI agents.

Jonathan Robitaille and Kevin Hytrek were the two agents assigned from the start to the task force. They were now part of the arrest team. But rather than fly out to Indiana with the Omaha cops, they were en route to Terre Haute at the moment by car.

Task force leaders decided the agents should now reroute south, locate Garcia and keep an eye on him. The FBI's freedom to conduct such interstate surveillance was one of the reasons the agents had been brought into the task force in the first place.

In the morning, everyone would wait and see what Garcia did. If he headed back to Terre Haute, the task force would be there waiting. If he continued to drive, the FBI agents would tail him and await further instructions.

The agents hit Salem in the fading light before dusk. They pulled off Interstate 57 and drove west on the main road, scoping out a Walmart parking lot and some other businesses.

Driving back toward the interstate, they finally spotted Garcia's car in the parking lot of a Comfort Inn motel.

The agents checked into another motel next door, carefully picking a room that would give them a clear view of Garcia's SUV. They also contacted the FBI's Springfield, Illinois, field office to request additional manpower to assist in the surveillance.

By the time the three Springfield agents had arrived and been briefed, it was nearly 1 a.m. And the agents the next day faced a potentially long day tailing Garcia. Hytrek decided the best thing they could do at that point was get some sleep.

"Be ready to start driving in the morning," Hytrek told the agents. They set alarms for 5 a.m., figuring Garcia wouldn't get on the road before then.

They figured wrong.

Hytrek awoke three minutes before his alarm went off and looked out the window. Garcia's car was gone. The agents scrambled. Hytrek called Omaha's Ratliff and asked for the latest ping location. He learned the last one still showed him in Salem. So if Garcia had left town, he hadn't gotten far.

The agents flew south on the interstate at speeds reaching 100 mph, scanning the road for a black SUV. They soon after got a new ping location from Ratliff.

Garcia was now in Benton, Illinois — a half hour behind the agents.

The agents flipped a U-turn to head back north, soon after spotting Garcia's SUV heading towards them in the southbound lanes. Once he was out of view, they whipped around again and maneuvered in behind him. They got their unmarked car close enough to confirm Garcia's license plate before backing off.

Mile after mile they drove, destination unknown. Garcia was seemingly in no hurry, driving 55 in the 65 mph zone and tailgating closely behind a semi truck. The agents hung 200 yards back and blended into traffic.

About an hour further down the road, Hytrek got on the phone again with Fidone. Garcia clearly wasn't headed back to Terre Haute. And they were getting close to the Missouri state line. If Garcia crossed out of Illinois, they would have to involve a new FBI field office and engage other law enforcement jurisdictions who knew nothing of the case. "We were running out of Illinois," Hytrek later put it.

Hytrek and Fidone agreed that Garcia shouldn't be allowed to leave the state. They alerted the Illinois State Police and requested they make the stop and arrest.

That's when Garcia again did the unexpected. Some 36 miles from the Missouri border, Garcia pulled off the interstate — right at the same exit where the two troopers who'd just been given the order to stop him were parked.

Everyone involved was taken aback by this amazing coincidence. Troopers Jeff Agne and Roger Goines were shocked to see the black SUV they'd just been ordered to stop suddenly driving right by them. And Garcia was clearly spooked at the sight of the troopers. Without stopping, he immediately headed for the on-ramp that would take him back to the interstate. Garcia only got halfway down the ramp before the troopers swooped in behind him with lights flashing. Garcia stopped.

Guns drawn, the troopers ordered Garcia out and told him to drop to his knees on the pavement. As Garcia complied, the troopers called out again, asking if he was armed. Garcia admitted he had a gun.

"I believe it's on the passenger side, if I remember correctly," he said. The troopers moved in and cuffed him.

Though it was still early in the morning, the troopers right away noticed the strong smell of alcohol coming from Garcia. A quick breath test showed Garcia's blood-alcohol level was double the legal limit. The troopers took him into custody and booked him for DUI.

The doctor, though, would soon learn he faced much bigger legal problems.

CHAPTER 18: THE RECKONING

Anthony Garcia was still settling into his cell in the county jail in Jonesboro, Illinois, when he was told he had visitors. Garcia didn't know them, but they were pretty familiar with him. Minutes later, he found himself face-to-face with Derek Mois and Scott Warner.

With Mois at the wheel, the Omaha detectives had hit the road that morning as soon as it was clear Garcia wasn't coming back to Terre Haute. During all the years they'd partnered in homicide, Warner frequently begged lead foot Mois to slow down. Not this time. They were hauling it. Both detectives were eager for the chance to question Garcia.

After arriving late that morning at the county lockup where Garcia was being held, they set up in an interview room. Soon after, Garcia was led in, dressed in the same blue collared shirt and dark slacks he'd been arrested in that morning. The doctor shook both detectives' hands. And for the first time, Mois sized up the man he'd been tracking virtually nonstop these past two months.

Mois was unimpressed. The homicide detective was used to suspects who came at him with a swaggering, in-your-face, fuck-you attitude. What he saw now surprised him. Garcia came off as meek and fragile, hardly a person he could imagine knifing four people to death.

"Dr. Garcia, we want to spend a little time with you," Mois said. "I'd like to clarify a couple of things. We're not here to talk to you about (the) DUI."

"We're here to talk to you about a case we're conducting in Omaha, Nebraska, and hoping you can help us," Warner chimed in with an affable, good-cop tone. "If you're willing to talk to us, we'd be more than grateful about that."

"Are you two police officers?" Garcia asked.

"Yes, we are," Warner said. "We're both detectives from Omaha, Nebraska."

"OK, ahhhhhhhh," Garcia said at the mention of the city of his past misdeeds. "I'll answer your questions — as long as an attorney is present with me."

And with those magic words, the interview was over as quickly as it started. The detectives had known going in that Garcia was likely to lawyer up. And any defense lawyer worth beans was going to tell Garcia to keep his mouth shut.

Still, the detectives' trip ultimately served another purpose. Mois had some news for Garcia.

After following the doctor back to the jail booking area, Mois told Garcia he'd be confiscating all of his clothes, wallet and personal items. They would be held in custody as evidence.

Garcia asked why. Mois dropped the news. "I have a warrant from Douglas County, Nebraska, charging you with four counts of first-degree murder and four counts of use of a weapon to commit a felony."

Derek Mois left his first and only meeting with Anthony Garcia finding the doctor's reaction to those words most telling. Garcia didn't get defensive. He didn't look surprised. He didn't even ask about the nature of the charges against him.

"Oh, OK," Garcia responded. And then without prompting, he walked himself back into his jail cell.

Standing in that Illinois jail at the moment, Mois wasn't sure Garcia grasped the hard realities that Mois now knew to be true. That Garcia would never spend another minute of his life as a free man. And that after Garcia savagely killed four people in cold blood, the reckoning had begun.

CHAPTER 19: MISSED OPPORTUNITIES

Late in the day that Monday, Omaha Police Chief Todd Schmaderer stood in the same room where exactly eight weeks earlier he'd announced formation of the task force. He triumphantly revealed an arrest had been made that morning in the Hunter and Brumback murders. Up on the screen flashed an image of Garcia's mug shot.

Speaking to a room packed with reporters and police personnel, the chief said he saw in the suspect "the elements of a serial killer."

"We did not feel this individual would stop unless an arrest was made," Schmaderer said.

Only an hour earlier, Dr. Bill Hunter had received a call from detective Doug Herout informing him the task force had just arrested one of his former residents for his son's murder. Up to that point, Hunter had been kept completely in the dark on who was in the task force's crosshairs. But now Herout told Hunter the name: Anthony Garcia.

"Oh my God," Hunter thought to himself upon hearing it. But that was quickly followed by another thought: "That makes sense."

Over all these years, Hunter had believed it just wasn't plausible anyone he'd worked with at Creighton was capable of killing Tom. He'd clung to that belief even after the Brumback killings.

Now Hunter knew the truth. Despite all he had done to help the young doctor back in 2001, Garcia had invaded Hunter's home seven years later and murdered his son.

In the weeks to come, Hunter would frequently question himself: How come I was so dismissive of him in 2008?

There would be room for other hindsight in the wake of Garcia's arrest. It had some second-guessing the police investigation, too. Had detectives missed a chance to crack this case sooner? Most importantly, could the Brumbacks' deaths have been prevented?

The answer to both questions was yes.

In the months after Garcia's trial, an *Omaha World-Herald* examination of police reports and detectives' interviews showed that, contrary to the public's perception of the case, Garcia's name was indeed mentioned to police — mere days after the 2008 Dundee slayings.

On March 17, 2008, four days after Tom and Shirlee were killed, Omaha police homicide detectives Eugene Watson and Linda Collins (then known as Linda Yetts) went to Creighton. Their task: Make contact with Angie Alberico, the coordinator for the Creighton University graduate medical education office.

Alberico had called Omaha police with a tip, wanting to provide the "names of certain medical students that were discharged from the graduate program. … Alberico thought that Omaha police should look into these individuals as possible suspects in regards to the Hunter and Sherman murder investigation," Watson wrote in a police report.

The Creighton administrator sat down with Watson and Collins and mentioned five medical residents. Two were Asian men who had been dismissed from the program; one the Russian doctor; another man who was kicked out of the pathology program for substance abuse. One other doctor was listed smack dab in the middle of those names: Anthony Garcia.

As with the other doctors mentioned, the tip was fairly generic, offering a limited explanation of why Garcia should be examined. Without any detail, the report nodded to allegations that Garcia and another resident had been partners in that May 2001 prank phone call — the final straw that got Garcia kicked out of Creighton.

"Alberico mentioned (the other prankster) who was in the Pathology Program 10 years ago as a person of interest," Watson wrote. "Alberico indicated a party by the name of Anthony Garcia who was originally from California and was also in the Pathology Program ... (and that) Dr. Hunter was the program director at the time they were enrolled."

That was it. Watson wrote down five sentences of general information on the Russian doctor; five sentences on another Asian doctor; three sentences on the American man; one sentence each on Garcia and his partner in the prank.

Then came May 11, 2008. Two months after his son's death, Bill Hunter emailed Collins "asking for advice about an upcoming article in the *Omaha World-Herald.*" A reporter wanted to run some information past Hunter. Collins advised Hunter "not to talk to the press."

But seemingly out of the blue, in the same email, Hunter mentioned to Collins "two individuals" whom he terminated seven years earlier — two people he had not mentioned in any of the interviews he'd given police two months before in the wake of his son's murder.

"Those parties were Anthony Garcia ... and (the other person who pulled the prank)," Collins wrote in her report of Hunter's email. Hunter had even listed those individuals' birth dates and Social Security numbers.

"Dr. Hunter stated these two residents were involved in unprofessional conduct and were dismissed," Collins wrote in her report. "Dr. Hunter stated that 'we were always professional with one another and I don't think they bore a grudge toward me.' "

That said, Hunter went on: "The reason that I even mention this incident was that several months ago, Garcia was disciplined by the Louisiana State Licensing Board because he lied on his application for his state license. When asked if he had ever been disciplined or terminated, he had said no."

Boom. Unbeknownst to Collins, there it was, in the black type on her computer screen: The name of the killer AND his motive. Provided by the victim's father.

However, despite that tip, and the other one two months earlier from Alberico, homicide detectives never zeroed in on Garcia.

In a 2018 interview, Collins said she remembered spending three or four days looking into Garcia in 2008.

Collins, who retired in 2012, said she found out that Garcia had lived in Louisiana. She went through a "very stingy" bureaucracy to try to get Garcia's driver's license photo, she said. And she sought records of any vehicles he was driving then. The car registered to him when he lived in Louisiana wasn't a CRV, she said.

Collins' recollections don't square with Omaha police records. Officials say no supplementary reports document any follow up by Collins or any other detective on the two 2008 Garcia tips.

It's also not clear why Collins wouldn't have found the Honda CRV registered to Garcia in 2008, given that Mois five years later received confirmation of it in the records he received from Terre Haute police.

As for motive, Collins said in the interview that she knew that Hunter had fired Garcia. However, she noted Bill Hunter was dismissive of Garcia — something he has acknowledged. Collins also recalled Hunter mentioning the job recommendation Hunter had made for Garcia even after firing him.

Collins said detectives in 2008 didn't comb through Garcia's Creighton personnel file, which would have revealed — as it would for Mois years later — other evidence of Garcia's grudge. Collins said they didn't do a deep dive in part because Hunter didn't think Garcia was the killer.

"You have to listen to the gut feelings of someone like Bill Hunter," Collins said.

The retired detective said she often prayed for guidance in her homicide investigations. "I feel God kind of directs you which way you should go," said Collins, a devout churchgoer. "I always felt I was a good investigator. I was very tenacious. I didn't want to give up until I knew we were at a dead end. … "And I really thought we had come to a dead end with Garcia."

In a 2018 interview, Omaha Police Chief Todd Schmaderer, who was not in charge of the department in 2008, said he understood in talking to others that Garcia's name came up "one time" back then but "he was not on the investigative radar."

A reporter showed Schmaderer the two police documents in which a Creighton administrator and even Hunter named Garcia shortly after the 2008 murders.

"The question really centers on, should he have been a focus or at least looked into?" Schmaderer asked. "My answer is yes. This was a very egregious crime. I would have liked to have seen that looked into."

It's not clear whether Garcia's name made it to the case's "lead sheet" — which sums up leads in the investigation and serves as a guide that police sergeants use to direct the investigation.

A review of investigative documents showed that Omaha police looked fairly deeply into a number of other suggested Creighton pathology suspects — including some seemingly less promising than Garcia. Collins spent six entire pages on the Russian doctor, one of the prime suspects. She also spent four pages on an African-American doctor; two pages on an American Indian doctor; and one page on an Asian doctor.

And her report suggests she and other detectives ventured far and wide as they chased the 148 various tips that had come in during the first two months after the killings. For example, Collins was assigned to interview a woman who had nothing more than a "premonition" in "a dream" that a 50-something guy had committed the murders. The woman mentioned a specific name of a man who lived in Minnesota. "The caller stated these thoughts are based on her nightmare and that she has no other knowledge of the case," Collins wrote.

Collins devoted 18 lines to explaining how she looked into the man in the nightmare. She devoted just six lines to Garcia, merely summing up the tips given to police.

The tips about Garcia fell into a mountain of reports that the cold case unit inherited in 2009. In time, the cold case unit would become knee deep in 2,300 pages of police reports. Garcia's name appeared on just five of those pages.

"It was a needle in haystack by then," Schmaderer said.

Ken Kanger, the head of the cold-case unit from March 2008 to June 2010 who went on to become the department's deputy chief, said his unit would have received all of the Garcia reports. But none of the detectives from the unit would recall seeing the brief mentions of Garcia in those reports or ever hearing his name.

Kanger said the initial investigation had so many tentacles — from Shirlee's daughter's boyfriend to the adults who played video games with Tom to the Creighton connections of both Bill and Claire to the FBI's speculation it was a serial drifter. They even spent hours on the phone with famed California criminologist Dr. Henry Lee, who meticulously went over the crime scene with them. Detectives followed all sorts of leads, Kanger said.

"We're talking about hundreds and hundreds," he said. "Obviously, afterwards, you always want to sit back and try to learn. You think, should we have spent all of this time on Tom's computer (interactions)? Should we have put more emphasis and resources on the hospital? There's going to be successes you learn from and there are going to be things you wish you would have done a little more.

"If we had got that right record and that right file that showed (Garcia's) vehicle, then you're right … it probably leads to a successful conclusion. But, I mean, I don't second-guess the effort. There was a lot of work done. It was, unfortunately, a unique set of circumstances that we hope we never see again."

At the time of Garcia's arrest, Sherman's family was among those critical of the investigation. They had long believed Omaha police weren't looking deep enough into possible Creighton connections, one of the reasons they hired their own private detective. "We're relieved they got the guy, but we're pretty upset, though, that two more people had to die before they solved the case," Brad Waite, Shirlee's brother, told a reporter after Garcia's arrest. "That's tragic."

That Garcia was able to strike again later didn't sit well with Schmaderer, either. The chief said it was heart-wrenching to think the Brumbacks could still be alive.

"We're human," the chief said. "Of course we wish it wouldn't have culminated in two more murders. It becomes personal to us in a lot of ways. And that drives us forward in every investigation that we have."

It would take the Brumback murders to bring Garcia into the fore. The day the Brumbacks' bodies were discovered, Hunter mentioned during an interview with detectives the incident in which Garcia was fired. He knew that both he and Brumback had played a critical role in the firing.

But at the time, some 12 years after Garcia had left Creighton, Hunter could no longer remember Garcia's last name, only recalling that he was Hispanic. It would not be until the task force began its dive into the Creighton personnel records — and Mois picked up Garcia's file — that Garcia's name would enter the investigation.

When Bill Hunter in 2018 was shown his 2008 email in which he mentioned Garcia, he took off his glasses and covered his eyes. He struggled to recall the time, and what prompted his email.

By May 2008, Hunter said, he had sunk into a "fog" of depression — and had given up hope that police would solve his son's murder. Police seemed to have no promising leads.

He may have come up with Garcia's name in response to continued police prodding for anyone or anything that might lead them to Tom's killer. If police had followed up on his email, he said, he likely still would have been dismissive of Garcia as a likely suspect.

"I had a hard time thinking it could be anyone at Creighton," Hunter said. "(Garcia) bore no grudge to me, or so I thought. We hadn't heard anything from him after he left. I just would not have been suspicious of him.

"I couldn't fathom who would do this to me or my family. I mean, I didn't have any enemies, I didn't think."

Hunter would later acknowledge it's possible his kindly nature and tendency to see the good in people left him with a huge blind spot when it came to Garcia. The fact that he now knew he had mentioned Garcia doesn't assuage any angst, he said, because it doesn't bring back the Brumbacks.

In the end, Hunter said, detectives faced a monumental task in trying to solve the killings. While in hindsight they could be faulted for not looking harder at Creighton suspects, and not pulling all the files, they had less reason to suspect a Creighton link in 2008. It wasn't until Brumback was killed that the Creighton pathology connection became obvious.

Hunter said he suspects investigating a crime is much like trying to diagnose a health problem.

In medicine, symptoms can be confusing and conflicting. Theories for what's wrong can be offered up, therapies can be tried, and still fail to offer a cure. Then a new symptom emerges or a lab test comes back, and suddenly the picture is crystal clear. Everyone slaps their foreheads and says it was so obvious. How could we have been so dumb? Why didn't we see this sooner? There's even a colloquialism for it in the medical world: retrospectoscope.

"I think that's what happened here," Hunter said. "Unfortunately, it took two additional deaths to make the connection."

CHAPTER 20: STRANGE WAYS

Though Anthony Garcia was locked behind bars, the Indiana State Police SWAT team still went in force to kick down the door of his Terre Haute home. They didn't know what dangers could still lurk inside. So in they charged, weapons drawn. In the end, what the tactical officers and Omaha detectives who trailed behind found on the inside was more bizarre than threatening.

While the attractive split-level house with the black Ferrari convertible pretentiously parked in the drive suggested a successful doctor resided there, the home's interior told a very different story.

Sparse furnishings, some rooms completely empty.

No bed, just a blue air mattress set on the floor.

Empty beer cans and trash as the primary decorative motif.

Amid the emptiness and disarray, a table with piles of papers set out at perfect 90-degree angles. They included Garcia's Utah medical degree, his Illinois medical license and the deed to the house he was about to lose to foreclosure — documents that spoke to a man putting his affairs in order.

Then in the kitchen sink, more papers in a plastic bag soaking in a strange, nausea-inducing chemical bath. Included were writings in Garcia's by-now familiar grade-school scrawl, expressing thoughts ranging from the incriminating to the bizarre. Read one of those hand-written missives:

"Invade (Rich House) —> Torture —> Murder —> Jack. Rich Children. Gun. Invade. Kill. Knife. Garage. Kidnap family. Torture. Kill."

As Ryan Davis, looked the paper over, the words seemed the ramblings of a psychopath: Antisocial. Homicidal. Completely lacking of any human empathy.

"This is something we are definitely going to want to take," Davis told Herfordt.

As Davis, Mois, Herfordt and other task force detectives in the days to follow peeled back the layers of Garcia's life by interviewing those who knew him and sifting through other evidence, they would uncover a stark and revealing picture of the failed doctor and the forces that drove him.

In sum, Garcia was a man who from the start never had the aptitude nor the desire to be a doctor, a career he felt pressured to pursue by his parents.

He was a man whose personal and professional lives completely unraveled into bouts of alcoholism, depression and thoughts both suicidal and homicidal.

A man increasingly detached from reality, his mind moving in ever more erratic, irrational and alarmingly violent ways.

A man who even after killing four people was still harboring vengeful rage for others he blamed for his problems.

And a man who when arrested was set for some dramatic act, the final move in an endgame only he understood.

"It really wasn't until we got to Terre Haute that we realized how twisted he was, as well as how messed up he was," Herfordt would later say. "Going into Terre Haute, we still thought he could have been some kind of mastermind gone astray."

Behind every killer there's a life story. Detectives, attorneys and others who probed Garcia's personal narrative would learn his years-long evolution from aspiring doctor to demented killer started where it all began for him: back home in California.

There, task force detectives served a search warrant on his parents' home simultaneous to the Indiana warrant. The Golden State detectives impounded and searched the silver CRV. But they also interviewed Garcia's family and spoke to neighbors and others who had watched the boy grow up. Getting beyond the medical school records, the detectives began to piece together the entirety of Garcia's personal back story — a tale of a family's lofty dreams that bitterly crashed into disappointment and failure.

Anthony Garcia was born June 9, 1973, in Los Angeles to Frederick Garcia, a postal worker, and his wife, Estella, a nurse. While Frederick had been born in the United States, Estella was a native of Mexico. The family at the time lived in east Los Angeles, the center of LA's Latino community.

Both parents worked full-time, so Anthony was raised by his grandparents until about age 3. That's when the Garcias moved out to suburban Walnut, where a brother, Fernando, and sister, Christina, were born. With a house in a tidy suburb, Fred and Estella were achieving the American dream. And they had even loftier dreams for their children.

Anthony was always a big kid for his age, needing to lose weight in order to play peewee football. He played in high school, too, by then perhaps with some pharmaceutical assistance. His family suspected he was taking steroids. Anthony eventually gave up the game in high school due to either a back injury or heart condition.

Even as a kid, Anthony seemed a loner. At no point in his life did it appear he was ever surrounded by an abundance of friends. There never seemed to be any women of note in his life. But socially, he did have a close relationship with his parents and siblings, and he wasn't one to get into trouble. There is nothing in Anthony Garcia's early childhood that would have led anyone to believe where he would end up decades later. By almost any account, he was blessed with the benefits of a very normal, loving middle-class upbringing.

From a young age, though, school often proved a struggle for the boy. By the second grade, he was diagnosed with a reading disability and nearly held back. The middle school years were tough, too. But the boy had some strength in math, taking every class in the subject his high school had to offer. He graduated from Walnut High School in 1991 with mostly B's.

Neither his grades nor his IQ, which was average as could be, suggested he was doctor material. But his parents, particularly his father, nonetheless had aspirations for their son. They pushed him to pursue a career in medicine. Not that the boy had any such desire. "Math was my favorite subject from first through twelf (sic) grade," he would write in a personal journal in about 2003. "I wanted to be a mathematician. My parents would not let me."

Garcia also had average grades in college before graduating from California State University-Los Angeles. And his score on the MCAT, the entrance exam for medical school, was low. Not surprisingly Garcia was no hot commodity as he started applying to medical schools around the country.

But of all the schools he applied to, one did accept him: The University of Utah. A school official later said that given Garcia's low grades and test scores, it's likely his ethnicity played a big part in his admission.

Garcia's father spoke proudly of Anthony as he went through medical school, at times referring to him as the family's "brain surgeon." Frederick Garcia often sported a blue "University of Utah Medicine" sweatshirt as evidence of his son's budding career.

In many ways, though, Anthony Garcia from the start was set up for failure. Tests later showed Garcia entered medical school reading at a fifth-grade level, and he was an extremely slow reader. Medical school involves enormous amounts of technical reading from texts and medical journals. Badly lagging peers who usually ranked at the top of their college classes, Garcia likely never had the tools or wherewithal to succeed.

"I read so slow I spend virtually all my time reading material over and over again," he wrote at one point as he sought special education accommodations from his medical school. "So much time is spent reading that I have no time to socialize, sometimes no time to wash clothes or dishes."

At Utah, he failed his biochemistry, physiology and human genetics classes and was forced to repeat them. He was put on academic probation. His mother later reported that whenever she visited him there, he always seemed tired, stressed out and depressed by his academic struggles.

Indeed, it was early during medical school that Garcia for the first time was treated for clinical depression. As another sign of his stresses, a citation for public intoxication suggests med school may also have been where he began drinking excessively. A psychologist later hired by his attorneys suggested one could see as far back as medical school the cascading personal problems that over time would combine to spawn a killer.

In Utah, Garcia also began to exhibit some of the personality traits that would dog him later in life. His teachers cited poor interactions with patients and staff. He was so rough with one patient during a OBGYN exam that he brought her to tears.

But somehow through the testing accommodations — and that extra fifth year — Garcia squeaked through to get his medical degree. He narrowly passed his national certification tests, too, sometimes after retaking them. He was now Dr. Anthony J. Garcia, M.D. And despite all his documented struggles, he even managed to gain acceptance into that family practice residency in New York.

In the summer of 1999, Garcia and his father loaded up an old van and drove straight through to that first residency at Bassett. One could only imagine how proud Fred Garcia felt as he left his son in Albany that day.

But Bassett, of course, became the first of three failed residencies over the next four years. As Garcia sought certification in a medical specialty — critical to getting his career off the ground — Garcia again appeared to be over his head academically. The blow-up with the radiologist that got him fired in New York came after he was frustrated about being interrupted while studying flashcards he'd made to help him muddle through.

After New York, Garcia landed back at home in California, seeming to his family exhausted, frustrated and not the same person they knew. But in July of 2000 came the second chance at Creighton. While there was clear evidence of stressors during his time in Omaha, it wasn't until Garcia's third residency in Chicago that Garcia appeared to reach a true breaking point, both mentally and emotionally.

In January of 2003, he showed up at an emergency room in Chicago complaining of migraine headaches and major depression. The previous day at work, he said, he couldn't stop yelling. He'd reached the point where he sat in his apartment all day crying, screaming, drinking and feeling hopeless, despite prescribing himself antidepressants, an anti-anxiety drug and a drug to dull his alcohol cravings. He also had fallen into a dark place, confiding to doctors he'd been having homicidal thoughts about his co-workers and thoughts of killing himself.

"I can't make the negative thoughts stop," he told his doctors. "It's like the thoughts aren't my own." For the protection of himself and others, he was hospitalized in Chicago for 10 days.

He was hospitalized again two months later with more suicidal thoughts. Now he was actually making plans to kill himself, expressing to doctors that he had thoughts of overdosing on his medications or stepping in front of a bus. As evidence of the seriousness of his condition, he was administered six rounds of electric shock therapy. Such treatments are often a last resort for treating chronic depression, after counseling and antidepressant drugs have proven ineffective.

By the end of 2003, Garcia had walked away from his Chicago residency rather than undergo an evaluation to see if he was fit to continue. He again landed in failure back home in California and holed up for the next three-plus years in his parents' home. The medical bills for his depression ultimately forced him into California bankruptcy court. He applied for and was granted disability income. Neighbors rarely saw him. His mom told them her son was "on vacation."

Thoughts of suicide persisted. One day, Garcia climbed behind the wheel of a car parked in the family garage and, with the garage door closed, turned on the ignition.

Minutes later, his brother came home to find Garcia passed out or asleep behind the wheel. He quickly stirred his brother and opened the garage door, foiling the apparent suicide attempt. Garcia denied that had been his intent, but his brother went upstairs to find Garcia's important documents organized for his family.

A note he scrawled in a notebook around that time also suggested the homicidal thoughts he'd expressed years earlier had not gone away. "100 years from now it will not matter. So kill them but do it right," he wrote.

As Garcia struggled with what to do with his life, he continued to apply for medical licenses — at least five states over time would turn him down, including his native California. But his parents told him it would be OK if he pursued another career.

He took some automotive technology classes. He tried to get on as a Los Angeles police officer. He applied to some law schools, though in at least one case he did so in an odd fashion, whiting out the word "medical" on one of his applications and changing it to "law." He explained in one law school application that he was no longer suffering from the migraines that had caused him to leave medicine.

"My health will not prevent me from completing law school," he wrote. "I discovered my flaw and it is not going to happen again. My goal as a law student is to fit in and get along with my teachers and classmates."

But Garcia apparently did not completely give up on medicine. And perhaps his struggles with depression sparked an interest in psychiatry. It's not clear how, but in the spring of 2007, he was accepted into the psychiatric residency at LSU.

Given all his struggles to find himself in recent years, the LSU residency must have come like a bolt out of the blue, offering Garcia and his family new hope. And for a time, it seems Garcia may have actually turned a corner. The reviews in his fourth residency weren't sterling, but they sounded nothing like those at his previous stops. One LSU faculty reviewer described him as "kind, well-mannered and intelligent." Another even remarked that he had "a nice personality."

But it all once again came crashing down for Garcia in February of 2008 when the Louisiana medical board uncovered his undisclosed Creighton firing. This time, his reaction to failure was different, as evidenced by his 730-mile drive to Omaha to kill Tom Hunter and Shirlee Sherman.

Why this latest failure turned a doctor who had previously never committed known acts of violence into a remorseless killer would remain murky even years later. Records from the time show in the weeks leading up to the Dundee killings he had been self-prescribing and injecting steroids, excessive amounts of which have been linked to anger, agitation, aggressiveness and violent behavior.

The best evidence of his dark mental state at the time of the March 2008 killings would come from a trip he took to see a California psychiatrist two months later. Back at home again with his parents after the murders, the 34-year-old Garcia once again slid deep into depression. He saw a psychiatrist in Glendale in May 2008, confiding he was having thoughts of hurting others.

"Never done that, it's just thoughts," he lied, according to the doctor's notes of the conversation. During the exam, Garcia reported feeling helpless, hopeless, worthless, angry, sad and withdrawn. While he did not admit to abusing alcohol, another doctor noticed hand tremors consistent with severe alcohol abuse.

But the Dundee killings had also not been an impulsive act. In the garage of the Garcia home in California, detectives found a duffel bag containing stacks of Garcia's old financial papers, dating to his life in Louisiana. These records would give detectives their first evidence of Garcia's calculated planning for the murders.

Detectives saw in the records that Garcia pretty much lived off his credit cards. He'd eat out three times a day, and sometimes visit a liquor store twice in a day. Curiously though, there were no charges made on March 13, the day of the Dundee murders. The records also showed that on March 12, Garcia had withdrawn $300 from his Shreveport bank — certainly enough cash to get him by for a couple of days on the road. Unlike with the Brumback killings five years later, Garcia back then was careful to avoid telltale credit card purchases during his trip to Omaha. It was more evidence that the Garcia of 2013 was in a completely different state of mind.

It was also noteworthy to detectives that before leaving Shreveport to head for Omaha in 2008, Garcia made an unusual $7 purchase at an auto parts store — a smoke-colored license plate cover. Such covers are illegal in many states. The reason: they make a license plate harder to read.

The credit card records showed Garcia was back in Shreveport within two days of the Dundee killings. A couple days after that, Garcia went out to buy more auto accessories, this time a new set of floor mats for the CRV. The detectives could think of some plausible scenarios why someone would need new floor mats after knifing two people to death.

Once back in California with his parents in the wake of the murders, Garcia would remain there for nearly a year. But then he somehow again found work in the profession he was so clearly not cut out for. By March 2009, the deficient doctor had returned to Chicago, where over the next year he was able to land a couple of odd medical jobs.

The work didn't involve anything particularly heroic, mostly performing minor health screenings. His employers would say he did decent work, though he was also described as a loner, with a wooden and odd personality.

The federal prison job in 2010 seemed to represent another step up for Garcia, enough so that he for the first time was able to buy his own house in Terre Haute. He also seemed at the time to try to get his personal life in order, seeking treatment in 2011 for alcoholism.

But by July 2012, he'd washed out of the prison job, too. Among the myriad conflicts which ultimately forced his resignation: he didn't like the fact he was supervised by a nurse; he came to work with alcohol on his breath; he left another boss some harassing phone messages.

Months later, during a weeks-long span in late 2012 and early 2013, Garcia got a double blow to his ego and future career prospects: he was denied an Indiana medical license and then fired from another contract medical job after showing up at a worksite drunk.

It was at that point Garcia seemed to become completely unhinged.

On a wild Jan. 5, three days after he was fired from his job, he showed up in a local emergency room with a blood-alcohol level triple the legal limit, saying he was suicidal. Five hours after being discharged, he walked in again even drunker than before. Before he could be treated, he pulled out his IVs and walked away. An hour later, he landed at another hospital.

"There is a part of me that wants to go home to the closet in my bedroom, get the gun out of the safe, load it and shoot myself," he said, according to his hospital records. Other than a month of sobriety, he said he'd been boozing consistently since 2004.

The three hospital visits that day marked the start of a series of interactions with law enforcement and medical personnel over the next several weeks in which Garcia displayed increasingly odd behavior.

A week later on Jan. 12, a Terre Haute fire and rescue team had to break down Garcia's door after he called 911. They found him on the floor surrounded by empty beer cans, a gun close at hand. They took the gun for his own protection and delivered him to a hospital. Three days later in a follow-up appointment with his doctor, he showed up drunk.

On Jan. 25, Garcia called 911 so drunk the operator advised him to call back when he sobered up. Five days later, he was in a car accident. Rather than waiting for police to arrive, he handed his entire wallet over to the other driver and left. The day after that he was back in the hospital, saying he just drank 20 beers. Three weeks after that, he asked a neighbor to call 911 because he'd lost his keys. When the responders told him he needed to sober up, he sat on the sidewalk outside his home and threw his coat over his head.

Not surprisingly, his cascading alcohol abuse finally got him arrested for drunk driving in suburban Chicago on March 12. "I am an alcoholic," he told the arresting officer. "I drink all day and night." It wasn't Garcia's only form of self-medication. He was also prescribing himself antipsychotic and antidepressant drugs. Somewhere in the midst of this personal implosion, it's clear Garcia became even more deranged, the homicidal thoughts intensifying. Just four days before the DUI, Garcia had gone to Gander Mountain to purchase the gun he used to kill Roger Brumback. Later evidence would also show this was the time he got on the internet to plot against Bewtra.

Garcia's odd behavior continued after the May 12 Brumback killings, as he lost a series of other medical jobs amid ever more peculiar circumstances. The strangest of flameouts came in late June. He showed up at an energy company where he was supposed to perform a series of physicals. Instead of going inside, he sat in his car eating and listening to music. He verbally abused a nurse who came out to inquire about his status. When he did come in, he asked one man to perform oral sex on him, challenged another to a fight, and then stomped off.

But the most telling evidence of how far off the deep end Garcia had plunged would come two weeks later, when the task force arrested Garcia and began searching his home and car.

As Davis, Herfordt and crime lab technician Amanda Miller arrived at Garcia's suburban cul-de-sac, they right away noticed the sleek Ferrari parked out front. But as the detectives learned, with Garcia it was all about projecting an image of success. A neighbor told them the seldom-driven Ferrari, as well as a Lotus that Garcia had recently sold, were always parked out in the driveway for everyone to see, even though Garcia's two-car garage sat completely empty.

His house was empty, too. "Well, this will be quick," Herfordt thought as he scanned the barren rooms. There wasn't much to sift through.

But he and Davis were immediately attracted to the eight stacks of documents laid out on the marble-tiled dining room table. This scene was familiar to them. For in addition to homicides, the detectives also frequently investigated suicides. It was common for them to see people who took their own lives first organize and arrange their affairs for the benefit of loved ones.

The detectives moved into the kitchen, where the cupboards were nearly devoid of dishes or food. The fridge was empty, too, save for some condiments and a box of cereal. "That's when we knew he was crazy," Herfordt would say later. "Who keeps cereal in the refrigerator?"

What most interested Herfordt and Davis, though, was a brown plastic garbage bag soaking in the sink. Herfordt went over and opened the bag, finding it filled with still more papers. "You need to stop that," Davis told him. "Can't you smell it?"

Actually, Herfordt couldn't. A medical condition some years earlier had robbed him of his sense of smell. He didn't realize that in stirring around the sink, he'd unleashed a powerful, nauseating odor. It appeared some household chemical had been poured over the papers in an amateurish effort to destroy them.

As in so many other endeavors, Garcia had failed again. While the ink on some papers was running, most were still legible. And in this toxic stew, the detectives would find still more evidence of Garcia's professional failure, financial struggles, mental decline, desperation and thirst for revenge.

Included in the paper cache was the detritus of Garcia's medical career, including lots of documents Herfordt and Davis were already well familiar with: Copies of the bad reviews he'd received from Chhanda Bewtra. The original letter Hunter had handed him when he and Brumback fired him from his Creighton residency. Reviews critical of his performance in medical school. Rejection letters from medical licensing authorities in Indiana and Kentucky.

Other papers spoke to Garcia's dire financial straits. There was a copy of a recent letter he'd written to his home lender seeking to stave off foreclosure, the letter saying he had not worked in more than five months. He'd been unable to get another job, he said, due to severe clinical depression, as well as his lack of board certification in a medical specialty.

There were also lists of ideas Garcia had drawn up on how he could dig out of his financial hole, from dropping his cell phone and selling all his cars to applying for public assistance. One thing Garcia didn't cut from his budget, though, was beer. It frequently topped Garcia's handwritten grocery lists.

As his financial woes grew more desperate, it appears Garcia's mind increasingly drifted to ways he could make money illegally. He searched on his computer for illicit ways doctors could make cash. The sink papers included information downloaded from the internet on how to commit identity theft. He'd even drawn up a rambling plan on how he could assume the identity of an Indianapolis man who also was named Anthony Garcia:

"Arrive about 10:30 a.m. when no one is around. Steal pertinent mail from mailbox. Where they shop. Super market, mall, movies ect. (sic) and shop with their stolen credit info/credit cards/ATM cards only at those places. ... Take out loans, credit cards, ect (sic) with their info. ... Follow him to work, ect (sic)."

Over time, Garcia's criminal plotting would become ever more incredibly dark and disturbing. Some of his writings alluded to kidnapping families, including references to "tie arms to sides" and "blindfold" and "use duct tape." Here's what his most detailed such plan said:

"Park around corner ... Common shoes ... Band-Aids on tips of fingers (doorbell) ... Fake drivers license ... Take jackhammer and crow bar ... Get their cell phones ... Separate rooms in house. Pawn furniture, jewelry ... Pin # ATM cash ... Plastic ties ... Sizzors (sic) ... Beer."

The Omaha detectives had always figured by the nature of Garcia's crimes they were dealing with some kind of psychopath. These writings seemed to reflect the thoughts of a man who would not hesitate to kill for his own selfish purposes. The old medical school maxim — first, do no harm — had become completely lost on this doctor.

But just how truly dangerous Garcia had become would be especially underscored the day after his arrest. That's when Mois, Warner and Miller ventured back to southern Illinois to go through Garcia's impounded Mercedes SUV. Among the eye-opening pieces of evidence they'd log:

A .45-caliber handgun and box of ammo.

A brand-new sledgehammer and crowbar.

A box of rubber gloves.

A road atlas containing hand-written directions to Shreveport, Louisiana, some eight hours directly down the road from where Garcia was stopped.

A stethoscope.

And, most chillingly of all, an LSU lab coat.

Mois' eyes widened when he spied the coat, with the school's distinctive logo on the chest. Why would he pull that out of mothballs more than five years after he'd been fired by the school? Along with the gun, maps and burglary tools, there was plenty of evidence Garcia truly was headed to Shreveport to seek more revenge.

Mois and Warner also found evidence in the car that it was all part of a grander suicide mission. In a blue LSU shoulder bag, the detectives found three manila envelopes that Garcia had addressed to his parents. Those envelopes were stuffed with more important documents out of Garcia's life, including titles to his cars and information on his life insurance policy. A note with the papers offered only this explanation: "Please hold these documents in case of an emergency. Your son, Anthony Garcia."

One personal list of to-dos in the satchel included "Destroy DUI and Justice (medical residences) and Bad info on myself" — a seeming reference to what Davis and Herfordt found soaking in the sink. Two other notes referred to Canada and New Orleans and could be interpreted as a possible suicide plan:

"Rent boat. ... Have fishing gear (look like a fisherman). ... In right hand: Gun (hidden) ... In left hand Phone, Passport, Driver's License, Poison (hidden), Knife (knives) (hidden), Cash, Mercedes Keys, Medications."

The road atlas with the directions to Shreveport also included directions from Shreveport to New Orleans, along with information on New Orleans businesses that rented deep sea fishing boats. Also, significant to Mois and Warner was what they didn't find in the car. Luggage. Not even a change of underwear. Garcia clearly wasn't on vacation.

As Mois and Warner processed the evidence taken from Garcia's car, they attempted to piece together his plan. Mois' best theory: His personal life now circling the drain, Garcia was on his way to Shreveport to kill LSU officials who had fired him five years earlier. The presence of both the lab coat and the burglary tools suggest he could have been targeting them in their homes or even in the halls of the school itself.

Then he planned to drive to New Orleans, rent a boat and shoot himself in a way his body would fall overboard and be lost at sea. That would then allow his parents to collect on the life insurance policy he was mailing them.

Parts of the theory would be further buttressed later when detectives listened in on a jailhouse phone call between Garcia and his parents. In it, Garcia told them he was headed to Louisiana to kill himself.

Regardless of what his specific plan was, there seems little doubt Garcia had dramatic plans as he drove his SUV south on Interstate 57. That was additionally supported by another paper Davis and Herfordt found left behind in Garcia's Terre Haute home.

The hand-written note featured words drawn from dialogue in "The Grey" — a movie released the previous year in which a group of men trapped in the wild are surrounded by a pack of wolves. In the movie's most climactic moment, the main character vows that if he's going to die, he'll die fighting.

Garcia's hand-written words likewise suggested he was now prepared for some kind of dramatic final stand.

Into the fight we go.

We live.

We die.

We live.

We die.

"Whatever his end game was," Davis would later say, "it looked like he was putting it into motion."

CHAPTER 21: THE NERD COP

Back at his desk in Omaha, Nick Herfordt plugged Anthony Garcia's iPhone into an electronic contraption not much bigger than a tissue box. Omaha's self-dubbed Nerd Cop was about to uncover what would prove to be some of the most damning evidence yet in the case detectives continued to build against the homicidal doctor.

Within three years of the iPhone's 2007 introduction, smart phone use nationally had exploded. Suddenly, almost every American was, in effect, walking around with a computer in hand — one that held such intimate secrets as who they were communicating with, where they were at any given moment, what websites they were frequenting, even how many steps they were taking in a day.

By 2013, law enforcement agencies across the country were slowly waking up to how critical digital forensics could be to police work. And few cops anywhere knew the cyber-sleuth's art like Nick Herfordt. If more criminals realized what digital detectives like Herfordt were capable of gleaning from a cell phone, they would never carry them.

"It's not rocket science," Herfordt liked to say of his craft. "But it is computer science."

Herfordt, though, was more than just a computer geek. What helped set his work apart were his investigative skills. He combined a detective's eye for knowing what type of information was most relevant to a case with the technical knowledge of where on the device to find it.

The little back box Herfordt plugged Garcia's phone into was known in the trade as a "universal forensic extraction device," or UFED — one of numerous electronic toys Herfordt had lying around his desk.

With the UFED, Herfordt downloaded all the data from Garcia's phone. He then ran the data through a software program, enabling him to navigate the byzantine numbers, letters and symbols that made up the code. He was looking for clues.

Herfordt first examined Garcia's internet search history, hoping he might find incriminating things Garcia had looked up on the web. The detective found only two searches there. Either inadvertently, or most likely in an intentional effort to cover his tracks, Garcia had recently cleared the phone's search history.

But simply deleting that history wasn't enough to foil Herfordt. For him, the browser history really represented just the low-hanging fruit. He had other tricks to help him find what he was seeking.

What Herfordt knew, and Garcia didn't, was that whenever a smartphone user closes out of a web browser, the phone internally saves the last page that was viewed in a mode called "suspended state." That way the next time the browser is reopened, the phone can take the user back to the same place. And, Herfordt knew, all those suspended state entries are stored. Herfordt went poking around in Garcia's suspended state log, and he quickly found a smoking gun.

He could see Garcia had gone on to the Whitepages.com phone directory website to search for the address of Roger Brumback. The log entry didn't have a timestamp, so Herfordt didn't know exactly when the search occurred. But again, Herfordt had his ways.

This new information prompted Herfordt to go to Apple with a search warrant to gain access to Garcia's account. After the court granted it, he went into Garcia's cloud account and downloaded all the information that was on Garcia's iPhone the last time it had been backed up.

Herfordt sifted through this backup data. To his delight, he saw it included all of Garcia's recent search history, before he'd deleted it. And it took him no time to find Garcia's search for Brumback's address. He had made it on Mother's Day, at precisely 2:57 p.m.

The day was obviously significant. And the time fit snugly into the Brumback murder timeline, coming right after Garcia's wing restaurant purchase and within an hour of when detectives believed the Brumbacks were killed.

Then came the biggest bonus of all: the data included the GPS coordinates for the exact location of Garcia's phone when he made the search for Brumback's address. The pinpoint put him in the parking lot outside Wingstop. In effect, Herfordt had just uncovered digital DNA showing Garcia plotting Brumback's murder right there in Omaha that day.

With this information, detectives now had a far more complete picture of what happened in Omaha on Mother's Day. After Garcia's failed break-in at Bewtra's, he essentially drove to the restaurant, ordered up some food, then got on his iPhone to track down Brumback as his next Creighton victim. It also helped prove Brumback was really just a fallback for Garcia. As he drove the hundreds of miles from Terre Haute to Omaha, the intended target was Bewtra.

That revelation, too, seemed to fit a pattern. Similarly, Mois and the other Garcia detectives would speculate that five years earlier, Tom and Shirlee also almost surely weren't Garcia's intended targets. Garcia had gone to the Hunter home either with the intention of confronting Bill Hunter at the door, much as he had Brumback, or to break in and lie in wait for Hunter, as seemed to be his plan with Bewtra. And then for whatever twisted reason — perhaps to cover up the fact he had been to the Hunter home — Garcia instead murdered an innocent boy and house cleaner.

With this finding, Herfordt wasn't yet done working his cyber magic. Looking at the search history on a laptop taken from Garcia's home, Herfordt confirmed that Garcia had been plotting his attack on Bewtra for months.

On Jan. 10, during Garcia's strange binge of drunken emergency room visits and four months before his trip to Omaha, Garcia had typed out a search for "home residence bewtra Omaha Nebraska." There were no such searches for Brumback, again underscoring Bewtra as his original target.

Around that same time, Herfordt found dozens of other searches that piqued his interest. Among them: "how to break into a house," "best crimes to make money," "breaking into a window," "credit card skimmer for sale," "how is identity theft accomplished," "ordering a fake driver's license," "how to make a pipe bomb," and "easy ways for physicians to make illegal money." All again spoke to the desperate financial straits that were driving Garcia to the edge.

Herfordt finally turned his attention to one other Garcia device, a Samsung tablet computer that Mois and Warner found in Garcia's car. Herfordt examined the tablet last because he didn't have much hope for it. In his experience, most people use tablets for little more than playing video games or watching movies.

But as detectives were increasingly finding, Garcia was not like most people. Herfordt soon discovered Garcia had actually done much of the final plotting for his Mother's Day massacre on the tablet.

Two days before Mother's Day, Garcia was up at 3:40 a.m. searching for driving directions to Omaha. Four hours later, Garcia had searched Whitepages.com for Bewtra's address and then mapped out directions to her home. Amid those searches, Herfordt also found evidence that Bewtra may not have been the only target on Garcia's radar at that time.

Just before looking up Bewtra's address that morning, Garcia conducted multiple searches for the home and work addresses of a pathologist who gave him bad reviews during his failed Chicago residency. As with Bewtra, Garcia had even mapped out the route to her office.

This was particularly significant for another reason: Detectives knew from Garcia's credit card and phone records that he had not traveled directly from Terre Haute to Omaha before Mother's Day, but had actually spent time in Chicago on the way there.

Herfordt had to wonder: Was this Chicago doctor even alive?

Herfordt reached out to her and found that, thankfully, she was still in one piece. It seems that if Garcia did indeed have plans to kill her in Chicago that day, that plan, too, had somehow fallen through.

The Chicago doctor remembered Garcia, simply saying, "He was not my favorite student, and I will leave it at that." Herfordt decided he'd leave it at that, too. With Garcia now in custody, Herfordt figured it was best not to cause this doctor any undue concern. He thanked her for her time and hung up, never telling her the reason for his call.

But that doctor wasn't the last potential Garcia victim Herfordt would discover as he followed in Garcia's digital footprints. Herfordt soon after found Garcia in 2011 had also looked up the home and office addresses of the New York doctor who had fired him from his Albany residency, a woman now living in Los Angeles. Garcia had even looked up her bio page, which included a recent picture of her, and mapped the route from his parents' home in Walnut to her office in Beverly Hills.

While the task force leaders had been concerned Garcia could kill again, even they might have been shocked to know just how many potential victims he'd been stalking. Between the Bewtras, the doctors in Chicago and Los Angeles and whoever he was targeting at LSU, there could easily have been a half dozen other murders had this pathological killer not been stopped.

The vindictive thoughts driving Garcia's homicidal plotting were perhaps best summed up by still more evidence Herfordt would uncover in his high-tech sleuthing of Garcia's iPhone.

One day Herfordt was sitting at his computer making random searches through Garcia's phone data, just to see what came up. Thinking about Garcia's motive, Herfordt typed in a word: r-e-v-e-n-g-e.

Up from the mountains of data popped a single hit. In February of 2013 — three months before his Mother's Day visit to Omaha — Garcia had opened the browser on the phone and typed in four simple words:

shall i not revenge

Garcia must have been trying to recall a quote he vaguely remembered from some long-ago high school or college English lit class. Because his search brought from the depths of the internet a quote from Shakespeare's "Merchant of Venice" — words from the bard that well summed up the reason for Garcia's cold-blooded killing spree.

"And if you wrong us, shall we not revenge?"

CHAPTER 22: ONE FINAL PIECE

More than a year had passed since Anthony Garcia's arrest. The Omaha task force had largely wound down its work and handed the evidence over to prosecutors for Garcia's upcoming trial.

But no one had more time and sweat equity invested in this case than Derek Mois. And rarely did a day go by in which he wasn't obsessing over some detail. Is there something we've overlooked? Is there more we can do? Have we done enough? "Even when cases are 'resolved,' I find myself considering what happened, what we did, what could have we done better, or sooner, items that we were never able to reconcile," he'd later say. "Cases stay with you. Maybe that's just me."

And one of the things that had continued to gnaw at Mois was Garcia's SD9, the gun that killed Roger Brumback. Mois knew from experience that if you're going to court to prove a homicide, it's best to have the murder weapon in hand.

The SD9 parts left behind in the Brumback home could not be specifically linked to Garcia's gun. When Davis and Herfordt searched Garcia's house in Indiana, they did find the original box the gun had come in. The detectives had the sales record from Gander Mountain, too. But they could find no sign of the weapon itself. After the Mother's Day massacre in the Brumback home, what did Garcia do with the gun?

The best theory was that he ditched it somewhere between Omaha and Terre Haute. Perhaps he threw it in a dumpster, a river or the weeds along the side of the road.

There were almost 600 miles between the two cities. That's not even needle in a haystack territory. But despite the long odds, like a dog with his jaw locked on an old shoe, Mois was just too stubborn to give up.

Contrary to what one might imagine, there is no comprehensive database for guns in the United States, something gun rights advocates vigorously oppose. The only searchable national database for guns is for those reported by gun dealers to be lost or stolen. Clearly Garcia's gun would not likely be listed there. Mois had gone ahead and queried that database a couple of times anyway.

Guns that come into the possession of law enforcement agencies also are not placed in any database. So even if another agency at the moment had Garcia's gun in hand, it was hard for Mois to know.

Despite all the barriers, one day in September 2014, Mois began to draw up a list of every law enforcement agency along the interstate between Omaha and Terre Haute. It was a massive undertaking, with dozens of municipal, county and state agencies. But Mois was prepared to reach out to them all, one by one, to see if they'd found the SD9.

Mois told Scott Warner what he was doing. They both agreed there had to be a better way. Warner later gave it some more thought. And he was struck with an idea.

"If another agency did get their hands on the gun, wouldn't they run the serial number through the database to see if it had been reported lost or stolen, just like we would?" he said to Mois. "Can we find out if anyone else has ever run the gun?"

If another agency had done so, Warner reasoned, that would be a tip-off that the agency now had the SD9.

It seemed no one, at least in Omaha, had ever thought about attempting what amounted to a search of the previous database searches. Mois took this idea to Kelly McDonald, the department data technician who handled such firearms queries.

That's not how it works, she told him. But McDonald also didn't dismiss the idea out of hand. She said she'd check to see what was possible.

The next day, McDonald emailed Mois. "There is one search that is not Omaha. Clark County Sheriff's Office in Illinois. Here is their phone number."

The technician had indeed figured out a way to search the previous queries. And as luck would have it, a rural sheriff's office in Illinois had run the serial number of Garcia's gun.

In July 2013, some two months after the Brumback killings, a truck driver had pulled off the interstate in Illinois, just across the border from Indiana. Nature was calling.

Looking down at his feet as he did his business, the trucker spotted the frame of a handgun — missing all its moving parts — amid the roadside gravel.

The trucker called 911 to report his find. The local sheriff's office soon after came out to pick up the gun, later running the serial number through the lost and stolen guns database.

The moment Mois saw McDonald's email in his inbox, he called Clark County. He was soon on the phone with the deputy who picked up the SD9. "Please tell me you still have the gun," Mois told him.

"Let me check," the deputy said, leading to the longest 15 minutes of Mois' life. But the deputy ultimately came back from the property room with the gun in hand.

Within days, Mois was on his way to Illinois to pick up Garcia's gun. He, Herfordt and two other detectives also went out to the interstate ramp where the gun was found and fanned out in the weeds and trees looking for more parts of the SD9.

In the end, they didn't find any. But the piece they had was the most critical, including the serial number that proved it had belonged to Garcia. Given it was missing some of the very parts found in the Brumback home, it would be nice to have at trial.

Mois had to chuckle about it all. He knew this was a gift. There were obviously a million better ways for a crook to ditch a murder weapon than dropping it right on the shoulder of the interstate. "He's not a criminal mastermind," Mois would later say of Garcia.

But even the biggest of murder cases, Mois knew, are built on lots of little things. During Garcia's upcoming trial, perhaps this gun could be the final piece of evidence that would assure justice for Tom, Shirlee, Roger and Mary.

CHAPTER 23:
COURTROOM COMBAT

Circles around his eyes — 5 o'clock shadow already appearing, by 9:30 a.m. — attorney Jeremy Jorgenson spun around in his chair. He craned his neck and looked around a courtroom pillar at the young woman who had just been led into the courtroom.

"Is that Celeste?" he whispered to the fellow members of Anthony Garcia's defense team.

A private investigator glanced at the woman in the first row. "You mean Cecilia?" the investigator asked.

"Yes," Jorgenson said.

"That's her," the investigator nodded.

Her presence set off a scramble. Jorgenson furiously whispered into the ear of Robert Motta Jr., another Garcia attorney. Motta snapped his head and looked wide-eyed at Cecilia Hoffmann.

The panic was a curious sight. After all, Hoffmann was destined to be a star witness during Anthony Garcia's trial. She represented practically the only witness directly connecting Garcia to the March 2008 deaths of Tom Hunter and Shirlee Sherman — once hearing words from him that were tantamount to a confession.

That she would testify to those words was no surprise; her potential testimony had been the subject of numerous pretrial hearings during the protracted three-year buildup to this sensational October 2016 trial. So the prosecution called her on the trial's ninth day. And amid her testimony, the defense asked to approach the judge.

"I'm going to need a recess," Motta said. "I mean we were trying to find out who you were calling. I mean, we asked, we texted (prosecutor) Don (Kleine). ... Who are you calling? It's hard to prepare for 70 witnesses."

Judge Gary Randall indicated he would dismiss the jurors early for lunch. Kleine was incredulous. "So let me get this straight," he said, "we're going to take a recess because they're not ready?"

He jabbed a thumb in the defense team's direction, typical of the fierce animosity that had developed over the past three years between the opposing sides. Motta glared at Kleine. "We have a client facing the death penalty," he shot back, "so I think a little time is warranted."

So court recessed. And courtroom observers were again left to ponder what normally would be unthinkable: Could the two sides actually come to blows?

Anyone who watches court will tell you that, while the U.S. justice system is adversarial by nature, a trial is a remarkably civil, even collaborative, production. The two sides may disagree on guilt or innocence, but they often agree on matters like what witnesses can be called or evidence presented, and work through any differences in a spirit of cooperation.

This case was different: cold and combative. It pitted a proud prosecution team from Omaha against a brash band of defense attorneys from Chicago.

Kleine, who turned 64 during the trial, was Nebraska's most experienced prosecutor — having handled more than 70 first-degree murder trials. A prosecutor for 30 years and the elected county attorney in Nebraska's largest county since 2006, Kleine was a Democrat known for his fearless prosecutions of gang members, serial killers, even police officers.

Kleine was joined by his longtime chief deputy, Brenda Beadle, a veteran of 20 murder trials. Beadle, in her early 50s, combined a detective's eye for detail with fierce drive and a storytelling knack. Sean Lynch, a junior attorney in the office, joined them at the prosecution table, back-stopping the lead attorneys.

On the other side was Team Motta, as it liked to call itself — Robert Motta Jr., his wife Alison Motta, and his father, Robert Motta Sr.

The junior Motta had never defended an accused killer, but his father had. As a young criminal defense attorney, Robert Motta Sr. was on the defense team that represented serial killer John Wayne Gacy. Gacy ultimately was convicted of sexually assaulting and killing at least 33 teenage boys in the Chicago area during the 1970s.

Bob Sr. went on to a productive criminal defense career — and came out of retirement just for the chance to try another serial murder case with his son.

Bob Sr. was as relaxed and folksy as his thick Chicago accent. Bob Jr. and Alison, on the other hand, were feisty and bold. The couple made their home in Chicago area courts, aggressively representing those accused of drug trafficking, DUIs and minor crimes. Perhaps their most notable case, before Garcia, was Alison's representation of an ex-wife who claimed R&B singer R. Kelly owed her money for child support.

Then came July 15, 2013. On a sleepless night, Bob Motta Jr. happened to check his work voicemail. Fernando Garcia had been randomly picking the names of attorneys out of a phone book and had left a message. His older brother,

Anthony Garcia, was locked up in downstate Illinois and needed an attorney. Right away.

It wasn't long before the Chicago attorneys blew into Omaha — and blew up any idea that they would adapt their style to their modest Midwest surroundings. Garcia himself was the first to offer a glimpse into the defense team's aggressive stance.

Typically, on the advice of their attorneys, defendants don't talk to the press. But here was Garcia, leaving a voicemail for an editor at the *World-Herald*. "My attorneys and I were talking — we're going to kick their ass," Garcia said in the call, not long after his 2013 arrest. "You can print that."

It wasn't hard to see where Garcia got his bravado. Three years later, Bob Jr. leaned across a table during jury selection for Garcia's trial. He eyeballed Kleine, 20 years his elder. "We're going to kick your ass," he said.

The comment was amazing in its audacity. Attorneys rarely make predictions, most simply saying they look forward to their day in court. In private moments, the Mottas' boasts left Kleine and Beadle incredulous. Prosecutors heard so much bluster that Kleine came up with an analogy for Bob Jr.'s chest-thumping.

Before the first Gulf War, Kleine noted, Saddam Hussein used to brag about how the Iraqi army would destroy "the infidels" from the United States. Everyone saw how that one turned out. Still, it all made Kleine a little uneasy. "It almost makes you wonder if he has something up his sleeve," Kleine said at one point. "Or is he just popping off?"

Say this about the defense team: They had little concern about what locals thought of them. Bob Jr. explained his philosophy to the judge during one pretrial hearing: "I don't practice here, so I can take a scorched-earth policy."

Once during another pre-trial hearing, Motta railed against Kleine. "I'm sick of his mouth!" It was just the latest of countless courtroom blowups that often had Motta screaming at the top of his lungs. During a teleconference hearing, Motta launched into such a screaming rant the judge repeatedly yelled at him to shut up.

Motta's wife, Alison Motta, was no less aggressive. A diminutive woman at 5 feet tall, Alison was a plucky and, at times, ornery attorney — outspoken and loathe to concede anything.

Garcia clearly was impressed with his attorneys' feistiness. The defendant often smiled, even chuckled, as Bob Jr. and Alison zigged, zagged and zinged their way through months of pre-trial hearings. But as the trial neared, the Mottas' mouths landed them in serious hot water.

On March 28, 2016, Alison Motta called Omaha news outlets, announcing that a defense expert had linked DNA on Shirlee Sherman's bandanna to another potential suspect. "The evidence conclusively exonerates Anthony Garcia," Alison declared.

Big problem: The DNA swab taken from the bandanna didn't provide a link to the man Alison mentioned. In fact, the sample was such a mix of various people's DNA it didn't implicate or exonerate anyone.

Prosecutors fumed. Kleine and Beadle suggested that Alison's comments were an attempt to poison the jury pool less than a week before trial. They weren't alone in their outrage. Days later, Judge Randall effectively booted Alison from the defense team. Alison would not speak at trial or sit at the defense table.

Alison's ouster caused the latest of several delays that would combine to push back Garcia's trial more than two years. Her role at trial would essentially be filled by Jorgenson, a mid-40s Omaha attorney who was the local attorney the Mottas needed on their team to be able to practice without a Nebraska law license.

Jorgenson had his own colorful background. He had tried his only prior murder case while his license was on probation from the Nebraska Supreme Court, a penalty handed down after he had accepted fees on a case whose legal claim had expired. But with the defense team set, Garcia was finally ready to go to trial in October 2016.

In any trial, the defense team is stuck with the hand their client has dealt them. That was doubly so in Garcia's case. In effect, the state had two major hands to play — one in the 2008 deaths of Tom and Shirlee, and the other the 2013 Brumback killings. Due to the similarity between the two sets of murders, Kleine had made the decision to try the cases together in a single trial.

When it came to fending off the charges in the Brumback killings, the defense case on its face seemed hopeless. Put simply, the state had vast amounts of physical evidence against Garcia in those 2013 slayings. Mois, Herfordt and Davis had been able to document Garcia's digital footprints in and around Omaha on Mother's Day. The task force also had a swab of DNA taken from Bewtra's door after the failed break-in, an analysis of which showed it had been left behind either by Garcia himself or a male member of his family. Mois had tracked down the murder weapon. Throw in the trove of incriminating documents found soaking in Garcia's home, and prosecutors could literally throw the kitchen sink at Garcia in the Brumback murders.

Contrast that with the scant physical evidence prosecutors had putting Garcia in Omaha during the killings of Tom and Shirlee: the fact that he owned the same make and color of car as the dark-haired, olive-skinned man seen around the Hunter home. Even that evidence was weakened by the fact that none of the neighbors had been able to pick Garcia out of a photo lineup five years after the fact.

The Mottas as a result knew their best defense was to win an acquittal on at least the Dundee slayings. For Garcia, such a feat might be the difference between life and death. A defendant in Nebraska who kills four people typically has a reservation on death row. A defendant who kills two people? Much less likely.

So the defense at trial took aim at the state's largely circumstantial case in the Dundee killings. And the state countered with its most potent evidence in those slayings: A stripper with a strange, remarkable story.

CHAPTER 24: RYDER

In the days after completing their search of Garcia's Indiana home, the Omaha task force detectives started hitting Terre Haute's strip clubs. They weren't looking for lap dances.

In interviewing people who knew Garcia, they had been hearing about Garcia's affinity for strippers. It wasn't a big surprise. They'd previously seen from his credit card statements that he dropped loads of money at strip joints. "We need to go to these clubs," Davis told Herfordt.

There were two strip clubs in Terre Haute, 6th Avenue and Club Koyote. What they had in common, Herfordt later said, was that they were "both absolute dumps." Club Koyote, which seemed to be Garcia's favorite, was set in a dilapidated, tan clapboard building in industrial West Terre Haute, with a sign out front billing it "The Wabash Valley's Sexiest Night Club."

There were also two kinds of dancers in Terre Haute, the detectives would find. First, there were the students from nearby Indiana State University, good girls who took to the seedy stage to earn money for tuition. And then there were what Herfordt termed the lifers, the girls who danced because they "wanted to get crank and get crazy." It was actually the lifers, he found, who tended to be most willing to talk to them.

When the detectives went to the clubs, all the dancers they spoke with kept giving them the same message: "You need to talk to Ryder." If anyone knew Garcia, they said, it was

Ryder. She was his favorite. And there was even buzz that Garcia had once said something to her about killing people.

Davis and Herfordt soon learned that Ryder's real name was Cecilia Hoffmann. It didn't take them long to find an address for her, a rental home in Terre Haute. While it seemed clear Hoffmann was one of the lifers, the detectives still feared she'd slam the door on them. But Hoffmann was quite welcoming, letting them inside and with no hesitation answering all their questions.

She told them how "Dr. Tony" spent a lot of money at the clubs, particularly on her. She told how he had creepily starting coming on to her, which ultimately made her decide she needed to push him away. And then she dropped a bombshell statement: In an effort to impress her, he once admitted he had "killed a young boy and an old woman."

During the interview, Hoffmann shed a lot of tears as she recalled that day. She had chosen to believe Garcia was just kidding, the reason she didn't report his words to anyone. Now these detectives were in her home investigating the very murders Garcia had alluded to. It hit home for Hoffmann that it really did happen. She had been that close to a killer.

Neither Davis nor Herfordt had a lot of hope going into the interview. By the time they had tracked Hoffmann down, Garcia was big news all over town. Would she make stuff up for the media attention? They had to wonder.

But now they were struck by just how powerful Hoffmann's story was. All the emotion and tears helped wash away their doubts. She came off as honest and sincere. They were convinced she was telling the truth. "Wow, I think there may be something actually to this," Davis told Herfordt after they left.

When the detectives got back to Omaha, they naturally faced the same questions from task force leaders. She's a stripper. Do you find her credible? Yes we do, the detectives assured.

Kleine and Beadle also soon came to realize what an incredible witness Hoffmann could be at trial. They knew full well that the case in the Dundee killings was legally thin. The prosecutors even traveled to Terre Haute to visit personally with Hoffmann. Not only did they want to assure themselves of her credibility, they wanted to establish a relationship with her. After all, they needed her to fly out to Omaha to testify at Garcia's trial.

At some point, though, it seems Team Motta set out to make sure that didn't happen.

* * *

Some two years after Hoffmann first met with Davis and Herfordt, the Mottas sent their own private detective to try to interview Hoffmann.

Steven Yahnke, a former sheriff's deputy, was a mountain of a man, standing about 6-feet, 6-inches. Court observers later dubbed him the "Amish Giant" because of his big frame, long beard and penchant for wearing a black fedora. With Garcia's scheduled trial at the time just a few months off, Yahnke in June 2015 stopped in unannounced at Hoffmann's home in Terre Haute.

Later accounts of the tone and tenor of that conversation varied wildly. The defense would cast it as a candid interview — a moment in which Hoffmann admitted she made up the whole story about Garcia. The prosecution would cast the conversation as a case of misrepresentation and coercion.

At one point as Yahnke stood inside Hoffmann's house, he put Alison Motta on the phone. According to Hoffmann, Alison said words to the effect of: "Honey, I would love for you to disappear."

Omaha police officers became aware of Yahnke's visit to Hoffmann before it even ended. Yahnke eventually said something that made Hoffmann suddenly question whether this imposing man who had flashed a detective's badge really was the police officer she'd been led to believe. She contacted Ryan Davis in Omaha, emailing him from her phone. Hoffmann told Davis there was a man in her house at that moment telling her she didn't need to testify at the Garcia trial. An alarmed Davis dialed her up right away.

"We absolutely need you to testify," he told her. Whoever this guy with the badge is, Davis continued, he certainly does not represent Omaha police. "If you don't know who this guy is, ask him to leave," Davis told her. "If he won't leave, you call the police."

Hoffmann ushered Yahnke out. But that was hardly the last word on the incident.

CHAPTER 25: WITNESS ON TRIAL

A striking woman with a thin frame and long reddish brown hair, Cecilia Hoffmann strode into the courtroom and took her seat on the stand. It was the morning of the ninth day of Garcia's trial — arguably the biggest spectacle in a Nebraska courthouse since Charles Starkweather went to trial nearly six decades earlier for his notorious 11-murder spree across Nebraska and Wyoming.

Not that Garcia treated his trial as if it was any big deal. Up to this point, the 43-year-old defendant had taken a silent front-row seat for it all. Dressed in a gray suit and glasses as the 16-day trial began on Oct. 3, 2016, he sometimes slept, sometimes feigned sleep, sometimes scribbled on a piece of paper, sometimes grumbled to the deputies escorting him.

Repeated psychiatric evaluations since his arrest had always shown Garcia competent to stand trial. But for reasons never explained, he never once spoke to his attorneys during the affair. Later, Motta Jr. marveled at his client's silence. "Think about being on your own death-penalty case and not saying a word to your attorney during the entire four weeks," he said. "To me, it's stunning."

While Garcia had the same uninterested look on this day, seeing Hoffmann take the stand — for the first time in three years laying eyes on his favorite stripper from back in Terre Haute — surely had to somehow pique Garcia's interest. Under questioning from Beadle, the 26-year-old Hoffmann soon began to testify to the pair's "relationship" from 2012 to 2013.

At Club Koyote, Hoffmann said, Garcia was gregarious. He flashed wads of cash and flaunted his medical degree. Outgoing and engaging, Garcia told anyone who would listen of his work as a doctor. "He was always laughing," Hoffmann told the packed courtroom. "He was really funny. We would joke around a lot."

Even so, Hoffmann said, there was something different about his big-timing persona. Most of her customers didn't want anyone to know they were setting foot in a strip club. She said it would take months for her to find out, for example, that one of her regulars was a real-estate agent, another, a cop. Not Garcia.

"He liked to flaunt that he was a doctor," Hoffmann said. "He wanted everyone to know that he was a doctor — that he had nice things, that he had a nice life." So much so that Garcia introduced himself to the dancers as "Dr. Tony." The dancers at Club Koyote soon embraced the nickname.

They had plenty of reasons to do so: Three nights a week, Garcia would drop up to $100 — no small sum at the dumpy club. A big spender like that would get his due. Whenever he walked in, the deejay would stop the music, lean into the microphone and bellow: "Hey everyone, let's welcome Dr. Tony to the club." As one psychologist who later studied Garcia would put it, Garcia was like a strip club version of Norm from "Cheers."

After arriving, Garcia would typically make his way to Hoffmann. She admitted she took advantage of the attention Garcia showered on her. A handful of times she texted Garcia, asking him to take her to Olive Garden, her favorite restaurant. He would always oblige. She wasn't interested in dating him, she said. She just wanted a free meal.

"It's not a good time of my life," Hoffmann explained to the jury, looking down. "It's not anything I'm proud of or happy about. I was obviously dancing. I was addicted to drugs. I drank a lot. It was just not a very stable time of my life."

Later, Bob Jr. followed up on the comment, asking her: "Nobody wants to be a stripper, right?"

"You'd be surprised," Hoffmann replied, a reference to some of her co-workers that elicited chuckles from the courtroom.

In addition to their scantily-clad dancing, Hoffmann said she and her fellow dancers sold attention and affection, often competing for the right to perform an erotic private dance for a big spender like Garcia. "As soon as he would come in, I would leave whatever I was doing," she said. At the same time, the attention from Garcia also stoked her ego.

"He would always give me compliments and tell me, you know, how pretty I was or how great I am, or things like that that just really boost your self-esteem and just made you feel good. He was actually very nice."

To a point. Aspects of Garcia gave her pause, Hoffmann said. "There was definitely something about him that you could just tell was off," she said. "Just this look in his eye or this face behind his smile."

Once, Hoffmann said, Garcia got down on one knee and proposed to her, offering up an invisible ring. The deejay called out: "Congratulations, Ryder and Tony, on your engagement."

Later, Garcia told Hoffmann that he had a dream that she had his baby. She politely laughed. Then Garcia pounded the dream story into the ground, for several weeks mentioning it every time he came to the club. "It definitely started getting creepy," she said.

Then came his creepiest tale. One night, as Hoffmann took a smoke break outside the club, Garcia joined her. Garcia had been pressing Hoffmann to date him. He had tried to kiss her after one of their Olive Garden dinners. She fended him off, telling him, "I don't feel like we're ready yet."

Now as they sat together, Hoffmann knew it was time to break away. Garcia was trying to get too personal. "Regulars, they start to wear themselves out," she explained in businesslike terms. "You've got to let them go. Let another dancer take over." But she wanted to let him down gently, she testified.

"So I started off by telling him, 'You're too good for me, you know, I'm a bad girl, and you're a good guy, you're a doctor, and I just — I like bad boys.'

"He just kind of looked at me and he said, 'Well, I'm not really that good.'"

Hoffmann paused.

"He said, 'Actually, I've killed people before.'"

Hoffmann said she challenged him. "Oh, please, Dr. Tony, I know you've never killed anybody before. And he goes, 'Yeah, yes, I have, actually.' And I'm like, 'All right, so — tell me about it.'

"And he goes, 'Well ... it was an old woman and a young boy.'"

At the time, Hoffmann testified, she thought he was just kidding around. So she went along with it, asking Garcia why he would do that. "He said, 'Well, they deserved it. ... Well, maybe they didn't deserve it, but I had to, and I feel bad.'"

* * *

Even courthouse novices who witnessed Hoffmann's testimony that morning could see just how damaging her words had been for Garcia. Motta Jr. in the ensuing cross-examination had a simple task, straight out of a defense attorney's playbook: Crumble the credibility of the person who heard the confession.

In other circumstances, that might mean grilling a police detective about his interview tactics. Other times, it means attacking a jailhouse snitch's shady background. For Motta in this case, it meant attempting to expose a stripper's deceptive ways.

Motta started off by revealing a few things about himself: He acknowledged he had been to a few strip clubs in his day — chuckling a bit as Alison sat just behind him in the front row of the gallery. He then told Hoffmann he wanted to get "into the dynamics of being an exotic dancer a little bit, because I don't know if the jury's ever been to a strip club."

"Kind of the goal for a stripper is to entice the customer into getting a private dance — that's one of the primary goals. Would you say that that's true?"

Hoffmann: "Yes."

Motta: "So I mean isn't it also true that a part of the job for being an exotic dancer is to create the illusion in the customer's mind that you're interested in them; true?"

Hoffmann: "Yes."

Motta: "So, I mean, you'll do things in terms of trying to get a regular to dance with you, you'll tell the guy that's not good-looking, 'Man, you're a good-looking guy,' right?"

Hoffmann: "Yes."

Motta: "So that being said, lying plays a big part — or deception plays a big part in your job; isn't that true?"

Hoffmann: "Yeah."

Then after casting Hoffmann as dishonest, Motta challenged the reliability of her recollections. Motta pointed out that Hoffmann admitted she had been drinking when she divulged Garcia's comments to Omaha police. And he pointed out all the statements Hoffmann had made to Yahnke that seemed to back off her original report of Garcia's confession.

Statements like: "I thought he said something and now I just think it's been too long and I don't think I was in the right state of mind to comprehend what he said." And this: "I don't remember what exactly the conversation ... was, and I don't feel comfortable enough to risk a man's life based on the bad part of my life." And this: "I can't stand by anything I said or did in that time of my life."

As Motta pressed her, Hoffmann struggled to come up with an explanation for her words to Yahnke. The best she could offer was that she didn't remember making those retractions. "I'm not saying that I didn't say (those things)," Hoffmann said. "I'm just saying I do not remember actually saying them."

No further questions, Motta said soon after. He surely believed that his pointed questioning had badly undercut Hoffmann's confession claim.

CHAPTER 26: BREAKING POINT

In this high stakes back and forth, it was back to Beadle, who had another chance to question Hoffmann. And she had some work to do with her star witness — her reluctant star witness.

Few people beyond Beadle and her fellow prosecutors knew at the moment just how reluctant Hoffmann had been to testify in this trial in the first place. After receiving a subpoena ordering her to come to Omaha, she went to court to fight it. An Indiana judge upheld the subpoena, informing Hoffmann she could be held in contempt of court if she didn't show.

So what did Hoffmann do the day before she was scheduled to testify? She missed her flight to Omaha. Beadle scrambled, panicked that Hoffmann might be bailing. She furiously called her. Hoffmann picked up. "What's going on?" Beadle said, feigning calm.

Hoffmann begged forgiveness. She had trouble getting her two young children to their babysitter's. But she still planned to come. Beadle wasn't convinced. In fact, she didn't know whether Hoffmann would show until she walked up the ramp at Omaha's airport. It was 10 p.m. She was scheduled to testify in 11 hours.

Beadle wanted to prep Hoffmann, to go over all the questions she might face. But she also wanted Hoffmann to get some sleep, to be fresh for the grilling she would surely face the next day. So the two just went over a few matters, and then Beadle had Hoffmann listen to a recording of the original statement she gave to Omaha police. "I didn't want to overload her," Beadle said later.

After having weathered Motta's cross examination, Beadle feared that Hoffmann might be nearing a breaking point. She had clearly struggled with all the questions about her inconsistent statements. Now it was the veteran prosecutor's job to rehabilitate her star witnesses' testimony.

Talking at a feverish pace, Beadle firmly rejected any notion that Hoffmann had spontaneously recanted what she'd told the Omaha detectives. She noted all the times that Yahnke led her with his questions. She also noted that Yahnke was asking questions in front of Hoffmann's boyfriend, who didn't know anything about her life as a stripper — a life she had turned away from in the two years between her Omaha police interview and Yahnke's visit.

At one point, Beadle noted, Yahnke had suggested to Hoffmann that she was too drunk to remember what Garcia said. "He put a lot of words in your mouth, didn't he?" Beadle said.

"Yeah," Hoffmann said.

"You've always said, 'I wasn't lying,'" Beadle said.

Hoffmann: "Yes."

Beadle: "You just didn't want to (testify)?"

"Exactly," Hoffmann said. "I was hoping I wouldn't have to do this. It kind of seemed like he was giving me an out."

Beadle jabbed a finger in the direction of Yahnke, sitting in the front row. She asked Hoffmann how she felt with the 6-foot-6 man towering over her in her house. "I was terrified," she said.

From the defense table, Motta audibly scoffed at the statement. As soon as Beadle finished her questions, Motta launched into his second cross examination, cutting loose on Hoffmann's words about fearing Yahnke.

"Scared of what?" Motta asked. "Did you think he was going to harm you? Is that what you're saying?"

Hoffmann: "I didn't know. I don't know. OK? It scared me."

Motta began yelling. "Really?! So you have a guy sit there at a bar and tell you that he's killed somebody, and that doesn't terrify you?!"

"Objection!" Beadle shot to Hoffman's defense. "He doesn't get to harass my witness!"

Judge: "Mr. Motta."

"So I'll re-ask the question," Motta said. "You're terrified of a guy who's showing you a badge that says he's a private detective ..."

Motta marched up to Hoffmann, his voice building to a scream.

"But YOU'RE NOT TERRIFIED WHEN SOME GUY TELLS YOU THAT HE KILLED PEOPLE?! THAT'S WHAT YOU WANT THIS JURY TO BELIEVE?!"

Motta's shrieking set off a din of simultaneous reactions.

"Objection!" Beadle shouted again.

"Sit down," Judge Randall implored.

Gallery members stirred uncomfortably.

The drama subsided. That's when Hoffmann quietly leaned into the microphone. In a soft voice, she answered Motta's question.

"When some pervert in a strip club tells me a joke," she said, "it didn't scare me."

At that, Hoffmann held a tissue to her glistening eye and dabbed at her running mascara.

Several jurors squirmed in their seats. One, a young woman, shot a cold stare at the defense table.

* * *

In the male-dominated arena of Nebraska courts — where men make up more than 80 percent of judges and more than 90 percent of criminal defense attorneys — the Garcia case was remarkable. Women stole the spotlight at every turn. Consider:

Dr. Bewtra and her candid and colorful critique of her one-time pupil, who she described at trial as "absolutely the worst resident in my 40 years of teaching."

The county coroner's physician, Dr. Michelle Elieff, taking jurors through a gripping, graphic, and authoritative overview of all four killings — one that critically showed the jury the striking physical similarities in the pairs of deaths.

Beadle, who standing alongside Kleine became the voice of the state's case, serving as narrator through every twist and turn. She gave a stirring opening statement in which she seized on the Shakespeare quote Herfordt found on Garcia's phone. She repeated it at key moments as she defined Garcia's motive for all the killings: his failure, due to his Creighton firing, to secure a medical license and steady job.

"If you wrong us," Beadle said again and again, "shall we not revenge?" It became the theme of the trial.

And then there was Hoffmann — clearly the trial's most potent witness.

Going in, it might have been hard to imagine a stripper — one who was even reluctant to testify — being a great witness for the state. But Hoffmann came off as both believable and resilient. "She was hugely important," Mois would later say. "I didn't have a lot of hope that she would come through. But she did."

Motta later defended bringing Hoffmann to tears on the stand, saying capital murder cases are serious business. But he likely didn't do his client any favors, particularly in the eyes of the jury. Because during her testimony, she had come off to the panel as a likeable, empathetic figure.

She told jurors how she had sobered up since her stripper days, kicking her addiction to alcohol, prescription pills and meth. How she now had a regular job to support her two children.

She had scoffed at Motta's suggestion that she wanted to testify in order to land a network TV interview. In fact, she said she changed her phone number in order to avoid reporters. Quite simply, she had no reason to concoct this confession. "I mean, I've gotten nothing — nothing good out of this," she said.

With the benefit of time and sobriety, Hoffmann said, she had looked back on her peculiar exchange with Garcia countless times. There was one thing she couldn't get past. If he was so full of bluster and trying to impress her with how tough he was, Garcia could have said he had killed some bad guys or drug dealers or someone in self-defense. Instead, he told her he killed an "old woman and a young boy."

During her time on the stand, Hoffmann had recalled the response she gave to Anthony Garcia that night:

"That sounds like the two most innocent people in the world."

CHAPTER 27: JUSTICE DONE

Jurors had deliberated only 7½ hours before the bailiff was notified they had a verdict, creating a stir within the halls of the Douglas County Courthouse. On the ornate, century-old building's upper floors, dozens of observers looked down through a wide atrium as nearly all the major players in this 8½ -year drama filed into Judge Randall's third-floor courtroom.

Garcia was up front with all the members of Team Motta, opposite the prosecution team the defense had clashed with so fiercely. His parents sat a couple rows behind him. The families of Tom Hunter and Shirlee Sherman also took up their places in the gallery. And sitting in the very back row of the courtroom, flanked by Police Chief Todd Schmaderer and the other leaders of the task force, was Derek Mois.

Mois didn't make a habit of showing up for the verdicts on cases he'd worked. But the detective felt compelled to be there for this one.

Cecilia Hoffmann may have been the most memorable witness in Garcia's trial. But no one spent more time on the witness stand than Mois — largely due to his Forrest Gump-like knack for being present at every important turn this case had taken. Dusting off his sports coats and ties, Mois was repeatedly called to testify on his ubiquitous role in the Garcia investigation.

On day one and day two, he described the abominable scene he found in the Hunter home in March of 2008, a boy and grandmother with knives impaled in their necks. He was called back on day three to testify to the carnage he walked into in the Brumback home five years later, and to the eerie similarities with the Hunter scene that he and Warner noted right way.

Then he took the stand again on day eight. On that day, he spent hours meticulously taking the jury through the winding path that brought him to Dr. Anthony Garcia: The black binder. The Creighton termination letter. The Honda CRV and pastel plate. The Iowa cell phone tower. The $7.69 wing purchase. The convenience store video. The SD9 on the side of the road.

Every time he took the stand, he faced a grilling from Team Motta, nitpicking his technique and conclusions. Mois always kept his cool. He didn't mind the scrutiny. In fact, he relished the chance to defend the work he and his colleagues had done.

Each time he strode up to testify, Mois would look into the gallery and see Claire Hunter, an ever-steady presence in the courtroom. Bill Hunter had avoided the trial, largely out of his family's concern that reliving the horror of Tom's death could reignite his PTSD. Other than when he was forced to testify on finding his son's body, and later to detail the events leading to the firing of Garcia, he stayed away. (The Brumback family likewise never showed any interest in being in court outside of testifying.)

But Claire Hunter and sons Jeff, Tim and Rob regularly took in the proceedings, even during what she'd later call "that awful, awful first week" — when the death of her son was graphically, painfully, detailed by Mois, the coroner and others. She felt compelled to be there. "I had to have all the facts," she'd later say. "I owed that to Tom."

When testifying, Mois would also never fail to note the presence of Shirlee's family, who also kept a steady vigil at trial. Shirlee's brother, Brad Waite, attended every pre-trial hearing and each day of the trial out of respect for the tough, hard-working family matriarch. Her son, Jeff Sherman, was also in court without fail, a man Mois considered one of the strongest people he'd ever met.

When you got down to it, these families were really the reason Mois was back in court for the verdict. All of his work in this case, literally thousands of hours, had been for them. And as was typical with Mois, he'd formed a close bond with them all. Mois had especially appreciated the phone call he'd received from Jeff Sherman just as the trial was winding down. "However this comes out, however it ends, I want you to know how I appreciate what you did and the sacrifices you made," Jeff told him.

Now, as Mois sat in the back of the courtroom, he was feeling an anxiety he didn't often feel. Mois looked again at Tom and Shirlee's families, seated just in front of him, and got a lump in his throat. Would these families hear the guilty verdict they deserved? What would he say to them if they didn't? How much more pain can they endure? Yet again, Mois questioned whether he'd done enough.

Sitting not far from Mois was Warner, who had also felt compelled to be there that day. Nick Herfordt wanted to be there, too, but made a conscious decision to avoid the courtroom. The reason? Had he been there, he probably would have punched Motta in the nose. "And I'm not joking," he'd say later.

Herfordt had testified at length during the trial about the methods he used to pull all that incriminating information off of Garcia's phone and computers. But Motta Jr. in response told the jury Herfordt had fabricated it all. That despite the fact Herfordt showed that after he found the information on Garcia's phone, he later went back to the original sources, like Apple and Whitepages.com, for proof that they had the exact same information stored on their servers. Had they made that up, too?

So rather than join the cops in the back of the courtroom, Herfordt sat at police headquarters following the verdict on Twitter. He feverishly updated his feed every few seconds, looking for the first media reports. Ryan Davis, who had testified at trial about the search of Garcia's home, had the day off that day and likewise was tracking the verdict from afar.

As the clerk prepared to read the verdict, Rob Hunter threw his arms around his mother and brother Jeff. Count 1 — the murder charge connected to Tom's death, would be the telling one. Given the weight of the evidence, if Garcia was convicted of that charge, he would likely be convicted on all of them.

In the tense courtroom, Clerk John Friend began reading the template language from the verdict handed down by the jury. "We the jury, duly impaneled and sworn to well and truly try ... do find said defendant ..."

Rob Hunter gripped the shoulder of his mother's gray sweater.

"... Guilty on Count 1, murder in the first degree ..."

Claire Hunter clasped her son's knee.

"Guilty of Count 2, use of a weapon to commit a felony ..."

Rob Hunter's chest started to heave.

On the verdicts went, straight down the line. With every successive guilty declaration, Rob gave his mother's shoulder a squeeze.

Behind the Hunters, Brad Waite wiped away a tear as his wife hugged him. Tears welled in Jeff Sherman's eyes, too. Beside him, Madison, the granddaughter Shirlee wasn't able to pick up the day she died, also cried. When her grandmother was murdered, Madison was just 6 years old. She was now a teenager, speaking to the family's long wait for this day.

For his own part, Garcia showed no emotion, only resignation. As the guilty counts rolled in one after the other, he cocked his head back to the left and leaned back in his chair, his left arm dangling off the arm.

Two rows behind him, his mother cupped a tissue in her hands, dropped her head into a full weep and leaned into her husband. Frederick lowered his chin. Seventeen years earlier, when he had packed up that old van to drive his son across the country to his first medical residency, who would have thought it would have all ended like this?

In the back of the courtroom, Mois felt more relief than elation. But he was so happy for the families.

Upon seeing the first guilty verdict in a Tweet from a reporter, Herfordt's first reaction was to text his wife to tell her he loved her. With all the time he spent away from home to do this job, he considered her support monumental — not just in this case, but in every one he worked. This was a poignant moment for him and every detective who had ever worked this incredible case.

As the judge dismissed the jury, Garcia rose from his seat. "You ready?" he asked the deputies before shuffling back to jail.

"The son of a bitch," Brad Waite said after watching Garcia leave the courtroom. "What I can't get over is how do you do that to a little boy? How could you do that to Shirlee, a grandmother who cared for everyone and wouldn't hurt anybody? To Roger Brumback as he answers the door? And Mary Brumback, the hell she went through as she fought him off. He didn't just kill them. It was torture."

Claire Hunter was surrounded by reporters and golden under the glow of TV lights as she exited the court. For all those years, she had desperately wondered who killed her son. Her conclusion after watching the past weeks' proceedings:

"They got the right guy," she said. "They got the right guy."

Minutes later, Claire gathered with the other victim families in a courthouse conference room. More than a dozen family members, representing four generations, cried and smiled and shared a bond borne out of the vile acts of one man.

Then the door opened. Kleine and Beadle and Chief Schmaderer strode into the room. And behind them followed a procession of a dozen task force detectives, among them Mois, Herfordt and Warner.

As soon as the Hunter and Waite families realized who had arrived, they broke into applause — a reaction that sent chills through many who were there. The long-searching families, the cops who finally cracked the case and the prosecutors who brought final justice home celebrated the verdict together.

There were lots of hugs. Smiles. Words of thanks. Laughs. And tears — not just from the families of the victims, but from the detectives and prosecutors, too. "You kind of let it go a little bit and say, 'OK, these families have got their answer,' " Warner later recalled.

All the attention made Mois a little uncomfortable. He'd never experienced anything like this. But he'd never worked a case like this one, either. He was quiet, saying little. But he was touched by the words and hugs from the Hunter and Waite families. It was special. The hardened homicide cop, so accustomed to seeing humanity at its absolute worst, months later again got sentimental as he put into words the genuine emotions that swirled inside him at that moment.

"I have a lot of feelings for those folks," he said, his voice cracking. "What I do, I do for them. I don't work for the chief. I don't work for the mayor. I work for the Hunters. And the Waites. And the Brumbacks. And everyone else who is left behind.

"I want to do right by these families. They've been through enough."

CHAPTER 28: EPILOGUE

The doctor turned serial killer was wheeled into the courtroom, shoulders hunched, eyes scrunched. He looked like he'd just rolled out of bed, his beard, hair and nails unkempt. And either sleeping, feigning sleep or in some kind of catatonic state, Dr. Anthony Garcia appeared completely oblivious to the proceedings as Nebraska's justice system decided he should die for his crimes.

More than 10 years — 3,838 days to be exact — had passed since the day Garcia calmly walked Dundee's quiet streets before ruthlessly knifing Tom Hunter and Shirlee Sherman. It had been 1,952 days since his return trip to dispatch Roger and Mary Brumback. But on Sept. 14, 2018, a three-judge panel finally decided the fate of Dr. Anthony J. Garcia, sentencing him to death for the quadruple killings.

The ruling came after his newly appointed public defenders — the Mottas were out of the picture by then, as Garcia could no longer afford them, financially or otherwise — made a case for why his life should be spared.

They conceded Garcia had murdered four innocent people. But they argued there were mitigating circumstances that should spare him capital punishment: That he was never cracked up to be a doctor, pushed into the profession by his parents, and then became drunk and deranged when he realized he couldn't keep up. Burdened by his profound failures, he came to fixate on the doctors he blamed for his troubles.

But the judges' panel didn't find any legal grounds in Garcia's sad personal story that could overcome the depravity and gravity of his crimes. The judges were unanimous in their decision to send him to Nebraska's death row.

Slumped in his wheelchair, Garcia seemed oblivious to it all. Not only did he continue to not talk to his attorneys, a silence he had maintained in the two years since his trial, he completely ignored efforts by his family to speak to him. "It appears Dr. Garcia is present to some degree," one of his attorneys said at one point as he glanced over towards the zoned out Garcia.

It would never be clear whether Garcia's listless, lifeless appearance was simply a case of him tuning out the world or whether it was another sign of the years-long, spiraling degradation of his mental and physical capacities. Hours later when he arrived at his new home in the Nebraska penitentiary, his official prison photo showed his eyes scrunched shut, a prison staffer holding his head up for the camera.

Garcia's parents and brother sat just behind him during the sentencing and showed no reaction at all when the verdict was read. They had long before resigned themselves to Anthony's fate. And they also for the first time seemed to collectively accept his guilt.

"He was just totally sick if he committed the crime the way they said," his father said. "He was totally mentally ill if it happened. He's not that kind of kid. To know my son went through medical school, struggled but got through it, and then this happened. I'm shocked."

Garcia's brother apologized to the families of the victims. "We hurt. We feel their hurt," he said. "We hope somehow they find some closure."

But for the Hunter, Waite and Brumback families, that was not coming anytime soon, if ever.

"That'll never happen," Brad Waite said. "When you have someone taken from you in such a vicious, inhumane manner . ... It will never happen."

Waite also accepted that it would be a long time, if ever, before Garcia paid for the killings with his own life. Garcia was facing years, even decades, of appeals. Just the previous month in Nebraska, a man convicted of killing two Omaha cab drivers was finally put to death by the state more than 40 years after his crime. "We'll get a sigh of relief upon his death," Waite said. "The sooner the better."

As Claire Hunter walked from the courthouse after the sentencing, sons Rob and Jeff by her side, she reflected thoughtfully on Tom and his happy, abbreviated life. He would have been 22 by that day, graduated from college, perhaps following in his parents' footsteps and enrolling that coming fall in medical school.

"It's hard to picture what he would be like," she said with a grin. "He should be remembered as a talented, playful boy. He was a joy in everybody's life. And he didn't deserve what happened to him by any means."

It was typical Claire. Even in the wake of the horrible tragedy, she and her husband had always focused on their happy memories of Tom. It was why even after the boy was murdered right there in their dining room, they continued to live in their lovely Dundee home. To them, it wasn't the place where Tom died. It was the place where their family had made their life and created so many joyous memories together.

Still, the loss of her son would always be keenly felt. Earlier on the day the sentence was handed down, Claire Hunter had told the judge of the impact of Garcia's ruthlessness on her family's life. She compared it to throwing a stone in a pond, ripple upon ripple arcing and spreading and touching everything in their path.

Indeed, the curious case of Anthony Garcia would long linger for all who lived through it. That would include the detectives who dedicated years of their lives to solving the crimes.

* * *

When detective Scott Warner appeared in court to hear the verdict against Garcia, he was struck by how much Tom Hunter's brothers had aged. "It was a reality check to see how much time had passed," Warner later recalled.

By then, Warner was no longer in the Omaha police homicide unit. He'd been promoted to sergeant and become a supervisor in the unit that worked with social service agencies in Omaha to protect children from neglect and abuse. Warner remained proud of the role he played in putting Garcia away.

"But that verdict was not going to change the fact Thomas was not allowed to grow up and become what he was supposed to, or that Shirlee's life was cut short, or that Roger and Mary were robbed of the chance to move on to a new chapter in their life," he lamented. "And for absolutely no reason whatsoever."

* * *

Even months after the trial passed, Nick Herfordt still fumed about Motta's efforts to impugn his integrity. He said he considered Garcia's attorney to be a worse human being than Garcia himself. At least we know Garcia was mentally deranged, Herfordt said. What was Motta's excuse? "He tried to say I was manipulating data," Herfordt said, "so he could get someone off who killed four people, including a child."

Herfordt could not have foreseen back then just how profoundly Garcia would impact his own career. For the Omaha police department, the Garcia investigation had been a game-changer, revealing just how critical digital forensics could be in gathering evidence and obtaining convictions. Mine the memory chip on that phone, and you never know where it might take you. Chief Schmaderer decided in the wake of Herfordt's cyber sleuthing on Garcia that it was time for the department to dive deeper into digital detective work.

Herfordt was named the full-time head of a new, standalone digital forensics squad, with two additional detectives and even bigger plans for the future. Herfordt moved out of his desk in homicide into a new lab, with still more high-tech gadgets at his disposal.

Soon, it became rare for Omaha police to work a major case that did not in some way come through Herfordt's unit. He was analyzing data not only from phones, but also fitness watches, vehicle GPS systems and electronic personal home assistants. In one 2017 case, Herfordt even used a murder victim's phone to solve a case, the location stamp on a photo the victim had snapped not long before he was killed helping Herfordt determine the identity of the killer.

"We really are just scratching the surface of what we can do," Herfordt said as he sat in his lab, set up in a former storage room at police headquarters. True to his offbeat persona, Herfordt refused to let anyone take the "Storage" sign off the outside door. He kind of liked it.

"I would like to have an office with a window," he said. "But I love my job."

* * *

Some might debate whether Anthony Garcia fit the definition of a true serial killer. But Ryan Davis, the Omaha police department's resident expert on the topic, had no doubt he did.

Well, Davis said, you start by the fact he murdered four people, and that the killings spanned five years. Garcia had a consistent motive. He planned the slayings out, utilizing a similar M.O. that evolved somewhat as he went along. He, of course, had his deadly signature, that knife to the jugular. And like many serial killers, he only stopped when he was caught.

"He was looking for that jugular vein," Davis said in 2017. "I think that was his way of saying, 'I'm a good doctor. I know where that anatomy is.'"

Davis spent another four years in homicide after the Garcia case, investigating dozens of other killers. But he said he would always take pride for the role he played in bringing Garcia to justice. He knew his hometown may never see another killer quite like him.

"It was a case that haunted Omaha for a while," Davis said. "It was a real whodunit."

* * *

As Derek Mois sat being interviewed by a reporter in a detective bureau break room, another detective butted in to grab some coffee. The colleague couldn't resist razzing Mois about all the attention he'd been receiving. Mois gave it right back.

Before he had helped crack the Garcia case, Mois was already inarguably one of Omaha's top homicide detectives. But after Garcia's trial and conviction, Mois became, in the words of one longtime department veteran, "a rock star." He, Herfordt, Davis and Warner shared Omaha's officer of the year award. Mois was prominently featured when NBC's "Dateline" and CBS's "48 Hours" aired news documentaries on the Garcia case.

Still, Mois was having none of the talk of his new celebrity. He was quick to point out he just happened to be the detective who first set foot in the Hunter home. The detective who by chance was on call when the Brumbacks were killed. And the one who for whatever reason was handed Garcia's binder. True to how he saw the world, Mois said it had not been fate. It had not been divine intervention. It was simple dumb luck.

"If any other guy in this unit had gotten the Garcia book, you'd be talking to them right now," he said. "Honestly, I didn't do anything that anybody in this unit wouldn't have done. I just got the right guy."

As much as Mois left his mark on the Garcia case, Mois would see over ensuing years it also left a mark on him — one that was as indelible as the sleeves of tattoos down his arms.

Years later, he could be doing almost anything when something, a sound, or a smell, would trigger it. A vivid image of Tom would flash into his mind's eye. "This is one of those that has always come back to me," he said in 2018. "I've always kind of felt I can't let that one go."

But in those moments, Mois would try not to think about the Tom he first saw when he entered the Hunter home that beautiful, awful day in 2008. He never wanted to dwell on the boy's final moments.

Mois chose to freeze time that day. To forever think of Tom in the simple moments before evil came calling: A bright, sweet and innocent 11-year-old boy, happily playing his video game into all perpetuity.

PHOTOS

Tom Hunter. Family Photo

Shirlee Sherman. Family Photo

BUS 185   - S   R*000
TU JAN 22 2008 02:17 48P MPH

Tom Hunter exits bus the day of his murder. Evidence Photo

*The scene detectives encountered when they
entered the Hunter home. Evidence Photo*

*Omaha Police stand in front of the Hunter home
in March 2008. Jeff Bundy/The World-Herald*

*Omaha Detective Derek Mois.
Matt Miller/The World-Herald*

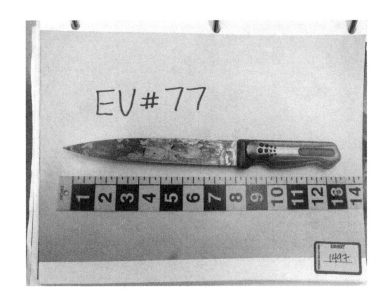

Knife used to kill Shirlee Sherman. Evidence Photo

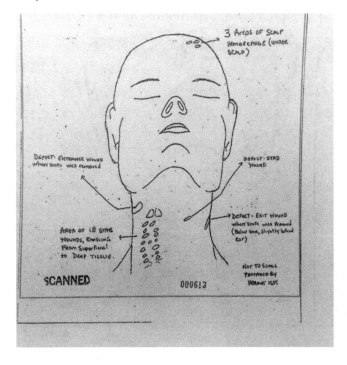

Shirlee Sherman's wounds. Evidence Photo

Dr. Bill Hunter talks a year after his son's murder. Kent Sievers/The World-Herald

Omaha Detective Scott Warner. Matt Miller/The World-Herald

Brumback crime scene. Evidence Photo

Screenshot of last FaceTime conversation between Roger and Mary Brumback and their daughter. Evidence Photo

The scene outside the Brumback home on May 14, 2013. Alyssa Schukar/The World-Herald

Omaha Police Chief Todd Schmaderer announces formation of a task force. Ryan Soderlin/The World-Herald

School of Medicine
Department of Pathology

**CREIGHTON
UNIVERSITY**

May 22, 2001

Anthony Garcia, MD
2575 Nicholas Court
Apt. B
Omaha, NE 68131

Dear Dr. Garcia:

You are hereby given notice of termination of employment for actions taken by you and Dr. Brian Nguyen on May 17, 2001 leading to the harassment of a fellow resident and his family and to the detriment of the Pathology Residency Program. Termination will officially take place 15 days from this notice, however, you are relieved of all patient care responsibilities at once and are to immediately vacate your office and not return. You are also to return all hospital and university property (including but not limited to ID cards and keys) immediately. You are further instructed not to attempt to contact, visit or harass any hospital or university employee or their families.

William J. Hunter, MD.   Date
Associate Professor &
Pathology Residency Program Director
Creighton University School of Medicine

Roger A. Brumback, MD   Date
Professor and Chairman
Department of Pathology
Creighton University School of Medicine

601 North 30th Street   Omaha, Nebraska 68131   (402) 280-4858   FAX: (402) 280-5247

EXHIBIT
1635

*Garcia's 2001 termination letter, signed by both Bill
Hunter and Roger Brumback. Evidence Photo*

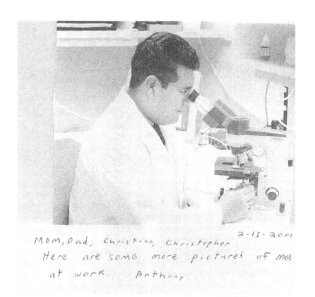

MOM, Dad, Christina, Christopher
Here are some more pictures of me
at work. Anthony.

2-13-2001

*Anthony Garcia during his pathology residency
at Creighton University. Evidence Photo*

*Frederick Garcia proudly wears a University of Utah
medical school sweatshirt, the school from which
his son, at right, graduated. Evidence Photo*

Omaha Detective Ryan Davis.
Matt Miller/The World-Herald

Omaha Detective Nick Herfordt.
Matt Miller/The World-Herald

Video captures Garcia making a purchase just outside Omaha the day of the Brumback murders. Evidence Photo

Garcia escorted by deputies during his trial on Sept. 26, 2016. Matt Miller/The World-Herald

Witness Cecilia Hoffmann enters the courtroom on Oct. 13, 2016. Chris Machian/The World-Herald

Douglas County Attorney Don Kleine, left, and prosecutor Brenda Beadle, after Garcia is found guilty on Oct. 26, 2016. Megan Farmer/The World-Herald

Garcia appears unresponsive during his sentencing hearing on Sept. 14, 2018. Kent Sievers/The World-Herald

For more pictures, go to:

http://wbp.bz/pathologicalgallery

ACKNOWLEDGEMENTS

Omaha Police Chief Todd Schmaderer had just announced the arrest of Dr. Anthony Garcia in the biggest criminal case to rock Omaha in decades. As a reporter for the *Omaha World-Herald* who had been on the story since the day Tom and Shirlee died, I followed Schmaderer back to his office right after the press conference. I wanted to pump the chief for more information that would be exclusive for our readers.

But I also posed another question that day in the chief's office: When the case wraps up, would he make his investigators available for in-depth interviews? At that moment, I didn't even know who those detectives were. But I had a sense that the story of how they had tracked a serial killer and unraveled the case would be a fascinating one.

Little did we know that it would take three years before Garcia would even go to trial, which needed to happen before we could get time with Schmaderer's detectives. Or that it would take another two years before Garcia was sentenced. But in the end, once I was able to sit down and meet the free-spirited Derek Mois, the quirky Nick Herfordt, and the dedicated Ryan Davis and Scott Warner, the story far exceeded any expectations. Their dogged detective work proved truly amazing.

Any acknowledgements in this book must start with those detectives who freely gave hours of their time to walk me through their work, in the process opening up emotionally on what the case meant to them. They are great representatives of the proud force they represent — thoughtful, truly vested and caring individuals. All of Omaha has been lucky to have them on the job.

We also must thank Chief Schmaderer for providing that access, not something every chief would do. And to thank the chief and command officers Mary Newman, Stefanie Fidone and Ken Kanger for offering their own insights into the Garcia case. Special thanks to Lt. Darci Tierney, the department's longtime PIO, for advocating for this project and for her everyday professionalism in working with Omaha's news media. Don Kleine and Brenda Beadle from the Douglas County Attorney's Office also shared with Todd Cooper the back story of all the legal maneuverings behind the case.

We owe much thanks to the Hunter and Waite families. I have been inspired from the beginning by their strength and perseverance. I in particular spent many hours with Bill and Claire Hunter. The Brumback family from the moment I wrote Roger and Mary's obituaries expressed a desire for privacy, which we always respected. But one of the things I loved most about this book was the ability to detail the personal stories of Tom, Shirlee, Roger and Mary — to show just what is lost when society breaks down and people kill.

In addition to those interviews, this narrative drew heavily from trial testimony, police reports, the previous work of World-Herald colleagues and that of other news media, including the 2017 documentaries by "Dateline" and "48 Hours." Special thanks to Judge Gary Randall, court reporter Sonya Kennedy and Kleine's staff for digging out evidence files upon request.

On a more personal note, I want to thank my family and my bosses at the *Omaha World-Herald*, including former publisher Terry Kroeger, former editors Mike Reilly and Dan Sullivan and current editors Melissa Matczak, Deb Shanahan and Kristine Gerber. And it was a privilege to work on this project with longtime colleague Todd, truly one of the nation's best courthouse journalists and a gifted storyteller.

We should never forget this entire project was grounded in the day-to-day work of local reporters. Books like this, and the opportunity to write them, are great. But I hope we never fail to appreciate the vital role journalists play in keeping the public informed, holding institutions accountable, documenting daily life and telling our community's stories. It is that every-day work that I take tremendous pride in.

Henry Cordes

For more pictures, go to:

http://wbp.bz/pathologicalgallery

*For More News About Henry J. Cordes,
Signup For Our Newsletter:*

http://wbp.bz/newsletter

Word-of-mouth is critical to an author's long-term success. If you appreciated this book please leave a review on the Amazon sales page:

http://wbp.bz/pathologicala

**AVAILABLE FROM JOHN FERAK
AND WILDBLUE PRESS!**

WRECKING CREW by JOHN FERAK

http://wbp.bz/wca

Read A Sample Next

CHAPTER ONE

TURNABOUT

Green Bay's television stations led off their newscasts with a chilling mystery on Thursday night, November 3, 2005. A fiercely independent, happy-go-lucky young woman from the heart of dairy country was gone. No one had seen or heard from her during the past four days. Television anchors painted a grim outlook as photos of Teresa Halbach flashed across the screen. Viewers were left uneasy and fearful of a worst-case scenario. Surely someone watching the distressing news would remember encountering Teresa over the past few days. At least, that's what the small-town Calumet County Sheriff's Office in Chilton, Wisconsin hoped.

But it was not Teresa's face displayed on the television screen that drew a red flag with one of the Manitowoc County residents. It was the image of her missing sports utility vehicle, a Toyota RAV 4.

During that time frame, Kevin Rahmlow lived around Mishicot, a small but proud Wisconsin town of 1,400, people of German, Swiss, and Bohemian heritage. Back in the day, Mishicot had six hotels, three general stores, a movie theater, a grist mill, and a brewery. By 2005, the community's three original churches still stood the test of time but Mishicot looked different. The town's gas station, owned by Cenex, was one of the local hangouts. People came there for fuel, a cup of coffee, and to buy their cigarettes. The popular business was at the corner of State Highway 147 and State Street.

Kevin Rahmlow vividly remembers when he pulled into the Cenex. It was Friday, November 4. Inside the convenience store, the missing person's poster caught his eye. Teresa Marie Halbach, the flier noted, was 5-foot-6, 135 pounds. Brown eyes and light brown hair.

"I remember that the poster had a picture of Teresa Halbach and written descriptions of Teresa Halbach and the car she was driving," Rahmlow said.

As it turned out, Cenex was one of many small-town businesses, bars, and cafes where Teresa's concerned friends and family slapped up posters. They were desperate for answers, hoping somebody, anybody, remembered a sighting. And if the locals didn't see Teresa, perhaps they saw her Toyota RAV4. It had a large Lemieux Toyota sign on the back of her vehicle where the spare tire hung.

When Rahmlow saw the poster, he remembered something.

"On November 3 and 4, 2005, I was in Mishicot. I saw Teresa Halbach's vehicle by the East Twin River dam in Mishicot at the turnabout by the bridge as I drove west of Highway 147. I recognized that the written description of the vehicle on the poster matched the car I saw at the turnaround by the dam."

That Friday afternoon, Rahmlow happened to spot a man in a brown uniform. The man was sporting a badge. "While I was in the Cenex station, a Manitowoc County Sheriff's Department officer came into the station. I immediately told the officer that I had seen a car that matched the description of the car on Teresa Halbach's missing person poster at the turnaround by the dam."

After speaking with the uniformed deputy, Rahmlow went on with his life.

He had no idea whatever became of the matter. He later moved to another Midwest state. He even missed the initial Making a Murderer craze on Netflix that captured world-wide attention.

***

In December 2015, a true crime documentary about the Steven Avery murder case was released on Netflix, but Rahmlow didn't get swept up in the media frenzy. An entire year passed before he finally turned on Netflix to watch it. And as he watched Making a Murderer, the Minnesota man had a flashback. He remembered his encounter at the gas station in Mishicot from more than a decade ago. And besides being familiar with Manitowoc County, Rahmlow knew some of the key people who worked hand in hand with special prosecutor Ken Kratz to cement the guilt of Steven Avery. Avery, as the world now knows, was a previously wrongfully convicted man who lost eighteen years due to a barbaric daytime rape along the Lake Michigan shoreline during the summer of 1985. This was the crime that allowed dangerous sexual predator Gregory Allen to get away by the forces who ran the Manitowoc County Sheriff's Office, notably Sheriff Tom Kocourek, who was about forty years old at the time.

Fast-forward to 2007. Avery stood trial in Chilton for Teresa's murder even though the prosecution's evidence was like a piece of Swiss cheese. And yet despite his side's many holes, Ken Kratz overcame his murder case's numerous physical evidence shortcomings thanks to the unbelievable eyewitness testimonies from a number of unscrupulous people who very much had a stake, a big stake, in the desired outcome of an Avery guilty verdict.

December 12, 2016

Two weeks before Christmas, Rahmlow sent a text message to someone he recognized from Making a Murderer. By then, Scott Tadych was happily married to Steven Avery's younger sister, Barb. At the time of Teresa's disappearance, Barb Janda lived in one of the trailers at the Avery Salvage Yard compound, a forty-acre tract out in the middle of nowhere surrounded by large gravel pits. At the time of Teresa's disappearance, Barb and Scott Tadych were steady lovers and she was in the process of getting another divorce, this time from Tom Janda.

After watching Making a Murderer, Rahmlow informed his old acquaintance how "I need to get in touch with one of their lawyers."

Rahmlow explained in his text message to Scott Tadych how he recognized Teresa's vehicle as the one he saw by the old dam, either November 3 or 4. He also remembered having a conversation with a man whose face regularly appeared during the Making a Murderer episodes.

Scott Tadych did not respond.

Rahmlow reached out again, ninety minutes later. The second time, he texted his phone number to Tadych. He wanted to discuss the matter over the phone.

"OK, I will I am really sick now can hardly talk so I will call tomorrow," Tadych texted back.

But Tadych never did call back.

"I did not hear from Mr. Tadych the next day or any other day responsive to my request for attorney contact information for Steven Avery or Brendan Dassey," Rahmlow said. "I received another message from Mr. Tadych on December 19 (2016) at 6:10 p.m., which was not responsive to my request."

There is no doubt in his mind that Rahmlow saw Teresa's RAV4 along the rural stretch of two-lane State Highway 147 near the East Twin River Dam. The turnaround on the highway was barely a mile from Avery Salvage.

A licensed private investigator in Illinois and Wisconsin, James R. Kirby was hired by Kathleen T. Zellner & Associates to investigate Teresa's murder case.

"I requested abandoned and towed vehicle reports for the time period of October 31, 2005 through November 5, 2005, from the following agencies: Mishicot Police Department,

Two Rivers Police Department, and the Manitowoc County Sheriff's Department," Kirby said.

This, of course, was the period when Teresa was last seen in Manitowoc County, near Mishicot. On a Saturday morning six days later, under highly suspicious circumstances, her Toyota RAV4 turned up, double parked, on the far back ridge of Avery Salvage, near a row of junked vehicles. The spot of the find bordered the massive sand and gravel pit operated by Joshua Radandt.

The question lingered. Who moved Teresa's SUV to the far outer edge of Avery Salvage? Was it the killer working alone? Was it the killer working in tandem with an accomplice? Or was it somebody affiliated with the volunteer search party? Or was it one of the Manitowoc County Sheriff's deputies?

Incidentally, at the time of her disappearance, Teresa's RAV4 had no front-end damage. This small but critical detail is substantiated by the fact that the missing person fliers made no mention of any broken auto parts or wreckage. But when her sports utility vehicle surfaced on the Avery property, it showed heavy front-end damage. Weirdly, the broken blinker light from the driver's side was neatly tucked away into the rear cargo area of the murdered woman's auto. Why would the killer do something so strange? Of course, the logical scenario was that the killer had nothing to do with moving the vehicle to Avery's property, and that the mishap occurred, late at night, during the clandestine efforts to sneak the vehicle onto the Avery property without Avery or his family members catching on.

In any event, private eye Kirby's inquiry into the RAV4 spotted by Rahmlow on Friday afternoon, November 4, 2005, revealed the "Mishicot Police Department had no responsive records. Based upon the response of Two Rivers Police Department and Manitowoc County Sheriff's Office pursuant to my request, none of these agencies logged an abandoned vehicle on Highway 147 near the East Twin River Bridge."

Obviously, one of the most plausible scenarios for why the police did not log the abandoned vehicle spotted near the Old Dam on Highway 147 in rural Manitowoc County, which was Manitowoc County Sheriff's territory, was because the auto belonged to Teresa, and it got moved as a direct result of Manitowoc County's intercession.

http://wbp.bz/wca

**COMING IN FEBRUARY FROM STEVE JACKSON
AND WILDBLUE PRESS! PREORDER NOW!**

SAVING ANNIE: A TRUE STORY by STEVE JACKSON

http://wbp.bz/savinganniea

Read A Sample Next

CHAPTER ONE-*The 911 Call*

March 16, 2009

Hood River County, Oregon

6:09 p.m.

When the 911 call came into the Hood River Sheriff's Office, it wasn't so much what the caller said, but how he said it. His voice neither rose nor fell as he phlegmatically relayed the information.

911 OPERATOR: *"911, where is your emergency?*

CALLER: *"Hello. I need help. I'm at, uh, Eagle Creek."*

911 OPERATOR: *"Okay, and what's going on there?"*

CALLER: *"My girlfriend fell off the cliff. I hiked back. And I'm in my car."*

911 OPERATOR: *"Okay. You're at the Eagle Creek Trailhead right now?"*

CALLER: *"Yeah."*

911 OPERATOR: *"Okay, and where on the trail did she fall?"*

CALLER: *"I don't know. I think about a mile up."*

911 OPERATOR: *"Okay."*

The 911 operator thought it was odd. That he was odd. Normally people calling 911 to report a traumatic event are in an agitated state with an emotional element in their speech ranging from weeping to a rapid-fire data dump to shouting or screaming. This guy might as well have been reading a manual on how to change a sparkplug.

CALLER: *"I hiked down and got her, uh, and I'm in my car now, and I don't know if I ... (unintelligible)"*

911 OPERATOR: *"Okay."*

CALLER: *"... suffering from hypothermia. I don't think it's that cold but ..."*

911 OPERATOR: *"Okay, so she fell off the trail down a cliff, and then you went down the cliff and pulled her, brought her back up onto the trail?"*

CALLER: *"No she's dead."*

There was a stunned pause as the operator absorbed his last statement; 911 callers in emergency situations tend to get to the point right away and gush with information. But this was more worried about telling her in his flat, monotone voice that he was cold than that his girlfriend had just died. And every time the operator tried to get more details about the victim, he turned the conversation back to his needs.

CALLER: *"I went down to get her. I went to the bottom. Then in the river (unintelligible) took me about an hour to get to her. I finally go over to her, then I was startin' to shake. I got too cold, so I'm, uh, now, I just got to my car, and I need someone to come and help me ... Please send someone I'm at, uh ..."*

911 OPERATOR: *"Okay, hang on just a minute ..."*

CALLER: *"... Eagle Creek."*

911 OPERATOR: *"... one second."*

CALLER: *"Okay."*

911 OPERATOR: *"And what's, what's your name, sir?"*

CALLER: *"Steve."*

911 OPERATOR: *"Okay Steve, what is, um ..."*

CALLER: *"I'm freezing. Will you please send someone?"*

911 OPERATOR: *"Um, hang on just one second for me, okay?"*

CALLER: *"All right."*

911 OPERATOR: *"Steve, what is your last name?"*

CALLER: *"Nichols."*

911 OPERATOR: *"And what's her name, Steve?"*

CALLER: *"Rhonda."*

911 OPERATOR: *"Rhonda's last name?"*

CALLER: *"Casto."*

911 OPERATOR: *"Could you spell that for me please?"*

CALLER: *"R-H-O-N-D-A ... C-A-S-T-O."*

911 OPERATOR: *"Do you need an ambulance? Do you feel like you might need medical attention?"*

CALLER: *"I don't know if I'm shaking from, I don't know ... I'm really cold."*

911 OPERATOR: *"Okay, okay, Steve."*

CALLER: *"I'm just really cold."*

911 OPERATOR: *"Are you able to start the car and get warm?"*

CALLER: *"Yeah, the ..."*

911 OPERATOR: *"Blankets?"*

CALLER: *"... car is running."*

911 OPERATOR: *"And now Steve, I know this is a difficult question for you to answer for me, but what makes you think she was deceased?"*

CALLER: *"I don't know it for sure. I stayed with her for about an hour and a half, and I gave her mouth-to-mouth, and I tried covering up her leg. There was blood coming out of her leg, and I just sat and helped her, and then I started shaking uncontrollably, so ... (unintelligible)"*

911 OPERATOR: *"Okay."*

CALLER: *"Had to go back, and ..."*

911 OPERATOR: *"Was she breathing when you left her?"*

CALLER: *"No."*

911 OPERATOR: *"Do you know if she had a pulse?"*

CALLER: *"Uh, no, I don't think so."*

911 OPERATOR: *"Okay, Steve, we have an officer who's on his way."*

CALLER: *"All right. How long ... how long will it take an ambulance to get here?"*

911 OPERATOR: *"It'll take just a minute. Would you like an ambulance for you?"*

CALLER: *"Uh, uh ..."*

911 OPERATOR: *"If there's a question, I can send them, and, um, then you can decide not to go with them if that's what you choose to do."*

CALLER: *"Just so cold. That's the thing, I'm cold. ... How long will it take to the police car to get here?"*

911 OPERATOR: *"They're on their way, okay? Hang on just a second. How far down the trail, how far over the cliff is she?"*

CALLER: *"Uh, I don't know, like a hundred feet ..."*

911 OPERATOR: *"A hundred feet, okay."*

CALLER: *"I don't know."*

911 OPERATOR: *"Steve, how old are you?"*

CALLER: *"Uh, 34."*

911 OPERATOR: *"I'm going to send the ambulance for you, okay?"*

CALLER: *"All right."*

911 OPERATOR: *"Hang on just a second for me. You're going to hear some silence, okay?"*

CALLER: *"Okay."*

The caller waited patiently and quietly for the 911 operator to get back on the line. When she did, she assured him that the ambulance was on its way and she would stay on the line with him until somebody got there.

CALLER: " 'kay."

911 OPERATOR: *"And we have an officer on his way from Hood River."*

CALLER: *"Where's that?"*

911 OPERATOR: *"Hood River? Um, it's about twenty minutes away, but he's on his way, about seven minutes ago, okay, and we have an officer coming from Corbett. Do you know where that's at?"*

CALLER: *"No I don't."*

911 OPERATOR: *"He's a little closer so he'll be there shortly."*

CALLER: *"Okay."*

911 OPERATOR: *"So I'm going to stay on the phone with you. Are you getting any warmer in the vehicle with the heat on, Steve?"*

CALLER: *"No but I have it on full so that should heat up."*

911 OPERATOR: *"Are you in wet clothes at all?"*

CALLER: *"Tried to ...* (unintelligible) *... up river. Uh, was too strong, so ..."*

911 OPERATOR: *"Are you able to get your wet clothes off and put something else warmer on?"*

CALLER: *"Yeah ...* (unintelligible) *... shirt off."*

911 OPERATOR: *"You what? You have warmer clothes to put on or dry clothes at least?*

The caller was silent.

911 CALLER: *"Steve?*

Still no answer.

911 OPERATOR: *"... Steve? ... Steve?"*

CALLER: *"Yeah, that helps. ... How far away is he?"*

911 OPERATOR: *"He said just a few minutes."*

CALLER: *"Okay."*

911 OPERATOR: *"Are you there?"*

CALLER: *"Yeah."*

911 OPERATOR: *"Hang on just a second for me, okay?"*

There were several more pauses over the next couple of minutes as the operator checked with law enforcement and the ambulance crew. Again, the caller patiently waited for her return and would then inquire as to when someone would be there to help him. He never once said anything about his girlfriend without being asked a direct question.

CALLER: *"What time is it?"*

911 OPERATOR: *"It's 6:18. They're going to be there in a few minutes, okay?"*

CALLER: *"Okay."*

911 OPERATOR: *"So Steve, how far up the trail did you say she is?"*

CALLER: *"I don't know. I think a mile."*

911 OPERATOR: *"Okay. What was she wearing?"*

CALLER: *"Uh, jeans. ... I don't know the top. ... She put on my shirt, but I think she put one over ..."*

911 OPERATOR: *"Okay. They're on their way, okay?"*

CALLER: *"Yeah."*

911 OPERATOR: *"Hang on one second for me, Steve, okay?"*

CALLER: *"Mm hmm."*

The 911 OPERATOR spoke to one of the responding officers: *"Brandon ... (unintelligible) ... responding? I have a hypothermic guy sitting in his car."*

The 911 OPERATOR then addressed the caller. *"They're on their way, okay."*

THE CALLER: *"Uh huh."*

911 OPERATOR: *"They're on their way. They said less than five minutes, okay? He'll be there in just a couple of minutes."*

THE CALLER: *"All right."*

The operator asked a few more perfunctory questions, such as date of birth for both the caller, January 4, 1975, and his girlfriend, July 2, 1985. The operator then attempted to gather more details about the "accident."

911 OPERATOR: *"Do you know what made her fall, Steve? Did she lose her footing, or did she get hurt? ... Do you know why she fell?"*

CALLER: *"I think she's high on something."*

911 OPERATOR: *"Have you done any drugs or alcohol today?"*

CALLER: *"No."*

911 OPERATOR: *"What do you think she's high on?"*

CALLER: *"I don't know. She always hides that stuff from me."*

911 OPERATOR: *"Okay. Are you doing okay?"*

CALLER: *"Yeah, I'm warming up a little."*

911 OPERATOR: *"Oh, you're ..."*

CALLER: *"Shaking. ... I can't stop shaking."*

911 OPERATOR: *"The ambulance is on its way. It will be there in a few minutes."*

CALLER: *"Uh huh."*

Again the 911 OPERATOR broke to speak to the responding officers: *"Are you guys aware of what's going on?"* After speaking to them, she returned to the CALLER: *"Did you leave anything on the trail showing where she went down over the cliff? ... Did you leave a backpack or anything there?"*

CALLER: *"No, I left my backpack ...* (unintelligible) *... farther down, so I could go down. But then when I made my way back up, I got it. ... Only thing I left was my sweatshirt."*

911 OPERATOR: *"You left your sweatshirt there on the trail?"*

CALLER: *"No that was down by the river. ... It's close to where she is, but that's where I went in the river. ... The policeman's here."*

911 OPERATOR: *"Okay. I'll go ahead and let you go."*

CALLER: *"Okay."*

911 OPERATOR: *"Okay."*

CALLER: *"Thank you very much."*

911 OPERATOR: *"You're welcome."*

CALLER: *"Bye."*

911 OPERATOR: *"Bye bye."(1)*

---

1. *March 16, 2009, Transcript of 911 Call From Stephen P. Nichols to Hood River County Sheriff's Office 911 Call Center*

With that exchange of pleasantries, the call ended. A young mother was dead. But the important thing, at least according to the 911 call, was that her boyfriend was cold.

http://wbp.bz/savinganniea

**AVAILABLE FROM BRIAN WHITNEY
AND WILDBLUE PRESS!**

MY SON THE KILLER by BRIAN
WHITNEY with Anna Yourkin

http://wbp.bz/mstka

Read A Sample Next

1

Anna

*The people I was with in 2012 mailed
boxes. It was not me—Luka Magnotta*

In the wee hours of the morning of May 30, 2012, I awoke
to a thunderous banging on the front door of my home. In a

panic, at first, I thought we were being broken into, but when I peered through the blinds, I saw that the street outside was lined with police vehicles and that there were several officers from the Peterborough Lakefield Police Service standing on my porch. I found out later there was also a team of officers in my backyard with searchlights, scouring my property.

I felt scared: why would they send so many officers to my home at that hour? I had no idea what was going on, but it was clear that whatever it was must be very serious.

When I opened the door, the officers asked me my name. Then they asked if Luka Magnotta was my son. My first thought was that something had happened to him, so I asked if he was okay. One officer said, "Your son's fine; we are trying to find him." Then they asked me if he lived in the home, if I knew where he was, and when I had last seen him.

I answered their questions and asked if this was about the "cat killing" videos that Luka was accused of posting online. I told the officers I had already been in contact with a Toronto police detective regarding that matter and offered to provide them with the detective's name. They didn't seem interested but wrote down the information anyway. They asked to see the last email I'd received from Eric, which was Luka's given name at birth. I also showed them the Mother's Day card that he had recently sent me. One of the officers pointed to a photo of Eric on my wall and asked if that was him. When I told him it was, he said, "He's not as big as I thought he was."

I questioned them as to why they were here, but the police refused to give me any further information about why they had come or why they were looking for Eric. They just told me I would know the reason soon enough.

At this point my daughter Melissa called to tell me that the police had come to her house at roughly the same time as they came to ours. She and my mother, who also lived at the house with my daughter, were hysterical. Melissa thought the police had come about the cat videos, as well, but was also told by the police that they couldn't disclose any information to her. One of the officers said to her, "Your brother is a very sick individual."

We were all very upset and confused. *What the hell was going on?*

Over the next few days, our nightmare would unfold.

I couldn't get back to sleep that night; my mind was racing. There was no way for me to get in touch with Luka. A few days earlier I had emailed him, and he'd said I'd caught him just in time, that he was closing down his email and that I wouldn't be able to reach him for a while. This wasn't unusual for him to say. He switched emails often. He also moved around a lot, and sometimes I suspected he wasn't living where he said he was. This was all normal behavior for him. He told me he was leaving for California, and he was very excited to start his new life there. He said he would contact me once he got settled. He'd been sharing his travel plans with me for a while, and although I knew I would miss him terribly, I was happy for him, he seemed so excited.

Throughout the day after the police visit, I worried constantly, hoping that Luka would contact me. I asked my mom and Melissa if they had heard from him; they hadn't either. I checked my email several times to see if he had messaged me using another account. Nothing. While I was on my computer, I happened to read an article about an investigation that was currently underway. It stated that a human foot had been mailed from Montreal to the Conservative Party office in Ottawa. Hours later a second suspicious package containing a human hand had been intercepted by Canada Post at a sorting facility nearby. Later, I saw on the news that a janitor at an apartment building in Montreal had discovered a human torso in a suitcase. It had been placed in the building's garbage pile. People were in a panic.

My mind started to spin out of control. I started thinking about the conversation I had a few months earlier with a Toronto police detective. He had viewed the cat videos and had found them very disturbing. He informed me at the time that this sort of behavior could escalate quickly to involve people. The detective and I discussed our concerns, and I provided him with important information as to where I believed Luka was then living. I was convinced Luka was in Montreal, not in Russia, as he had wanted us all to believe. A Mother's Day card he had sent was postmarked from Montreal and had contained a Quebec lottery ticket. Luka tried to cover that up by saying he had a friend from Montreal send it to me, but the card was in his handwriting. I'd offered to give the detective the card and ticket to assist them in finding him. I figured they could locate the lottery terminal and the store where the ticket was purchased and find the location the letter was mailed from. The detective declined my offer, stating my information wouldn't be much help.

With all this running through my head, I had a dreadful thought. Could it be my son, Luka, whom they were looking for in connection with this crime? Had he killed someone? It started to become impossible to escape this thought.

I was a nervous wreck. Over the following days, I desperately hoped to hear from my son, but there was still no word from him.

The months leading up to this time had been rough for me; my partner at the time, Leo Sr., had been making my life a living hell since I'd agreed to let him move back home that March. He was arrested for assaulting me in June 2010, and we lived apart until March of 2012 when I made the mistake of letting him come home. The night the police came looking for Luka was no different. Leo Sr. kept me up most of the night, tormenting me, as usual. He kept putting Luka down, telling me I was useless, complaining about things in the past and ranting about finances. It was a horrible night, and I was a mess by morning. Somehow, I got my two youngest children, Leo and Leeanna, off to school. Shortly after I got back from dropping them off, my son Conrad who was twenty-eight at the time came over, as he often did, to keep me company. I loved having him around because I felt safe from Leo Sr. when Conrad was with me. Conrad and I began chatting, and I felt compelled to tell him about my dreadful thought. He was shocked, and told me, "No, Mom, Eric wouldn't do that, it's not him! Why would you even think that?" I explained my reasons and told him I heard there was going to be a news conference on TV with more information, and I was going to watch it.

That afternoon when I turned on the TV, the news conference was already underway. It was broadcast on several channels; we watched it on CNN. The reporter was recapping footage of the crime scene in Montreal. We saw shots of police officers carrying large yellow evidence bags. Commander Ian Lafrenière of the Montreal Police was interviewed, and he stated that after scouring the crime scene in Montreal, police had discovered papers identifying the suspect, and they were going to release the person's name and photo shortly. As I watched this gruesome story unfold before my eyes, I started to become petrified. Seeing this on the news at any given time would have sickened me, but with my dreadful thought looming over me, I was in an absolute state of panic. I started repeating over and over to myself, "It's not Luka. It's not Luka. It's someone else. They'll reveal the suspect's identity soon, and this will all be over!" But in truth, I was scared to death. Conrad kept saying, "Mom, stop, calm down, it's not him."

It seemed to take forever, but when they were finally ready to name the suspect, I got up and stood in front of the television. My heart was pounding, and I started to shake. I kept repeating, "Oh please let me be wrong!" The first bit of information to come onto the screen was a silhouette of a male. They then reported that the suspect was a twenty-nine-year-old male. Luka was twenty-nine! I started nervously shifting from one foot to the other, holding my hands to my mouth, so I wouldn't cry out or scream. Then they flashed up the suspect's photo and name. My knees gave out, and I started to fall. Conrad grabbed me and held me in his arms as I sobbed uncontrollably. I cried out in horror, "No, no, no this isn't happening!" over and over again. Conrad was shaking, too, as we held each other. He tried to be strong and tried to console me, but we were both in shock and absolutely devastated. As newscasters continued to talk we heard them say that a warrant for first-degree murder had been issued.

It felt like I was trapped in a horrible nightmare. *Is this real?* I thought. *It can't be!* My head was spinning as I tried to take in what was happening. Leo Sr. sat there smirking at me through it all, saying things like "It doesn't surprise me." He almost seemed happy. All of a sudden, the phone started ringing non-stop. I felt I needed to call my parents, and I wanted my other four children with me. But the two youngest, Leo and Leeanna, were at school, and Melissa was still out of town.

When I called my parents, my father had already heard the news. He was beyond devastated and at a loss for words. My mother was so confused and distraught that she thought Luka was the one who had been murdered. When she finally understood that it was Luka who was wanted for murder. I thought she was going to die. Her voice was shaking, and she was screaming, "Why? Are you sure? No! What are you going to do?"

I had to call Melissa; I knew she hadn't heard the news yet, or she would have called me by now. I dialed her number and mustered up enough strength to remain calm. I asked if she was okay, where she was, and when she would be home. She said she was on her way and she would be back in Peterborough in an hour or two. I prayed she wouldn't hear the news while driving. Conrad and I tended to my poor little granddaughter Emily. She could sense the turmoil in the house, and she was very upset. I didn't want my granddaughter to see me so distraught. I sat and rocked her in my arms, and as she cried on my shoulder, I sobbed silent tears. Leo Jr. and Leeanna, who were thirteen and fifteen at the time, came home from school and wanted to know what was wrong. Conrad and I were speechless. We didn't know what to tell them. Still crying and shaking, we did the only thing we could think of. We told them to come and sit down in the living room, and we turned up the television and told them to watch. It was better they found it out this way than when no family was around. Like the rest of us, they couldn't believe what they were hearing and seeing. They were in shock. They flooded us with a multitude of questions for which we didn't have the answers. Conrad and I went to the kids, and we all embraced one another in a circle. As my world was falling apart around me, Leo Sr. was still taunting me with cruel comments. Unbelievably, he was taping the news broadcasts. He played parts of them over and over again, switching back and forth from the PVR to live television. I called Melissa a few more times to check on her whereabouts. She kept asking, "Is Emily okay? Is anything wrong? Why do you keep calling me?" I remained as calm as I could and said, "Just checking to see where you are." She still hadn't heard the news, and I was worried sick she'd hear it in the car. I couldn't wait for her to get home.

The phone continued to ring off the hook all afternoon: it was mostly reporters wanting a story. A knock came at the door. It was the Peterborough Police. They had planned on breaking the news to me before the story aired, they said, but they were too late. They explained to me that this was the reason they had come to the house the other night. They had been asked to come by the Montreal Police, but they hadn't been able to give me any information at the time as the investigation had just begun. I remember the officer asking me if I was okay, and I replied, "No, and I never will be!" They kept asking us questions. I can't even remember most of what they said. Conrad was handling it all at that point. I felt physically ill and wanted to just lie down, curl up in a ball, and go to sleep. It felt like I was in a horrible nightmare, and I just wanted to wake up. The police didn't stay long, and soon after they left, Melissa arrived home. She knew instantly that something was terribly wrong. I grabbed my daughter and just hugged her. Melissa was the sibling who had always had the closest relationship with Eric, and I knew this would be hard for her to hear. She said, "Mommy, what's going on? What's wrong?"

Conrad and I pointed to the television and I said, "Sit down." As she watched in silent horror, her face went white. Conrad and I wrapped our arms around her and just held her. Just like the rest of us she was in shock and couldn't believe it. We all had so many questions, but the only information we had was what was being broadcast on the television.

Then the media frenzy hit, and we were swarmed. Reporters started pounding on our door, cameras in hand. We were polite with them at first, asking them to please go away and leave us alone. We repeated the words, "No comment" over and over and over again. But they were relentless. They camped out in the street in vans in front of our house. There were reporters with cameras and tripods set up; they were in the neighbors' yards, some were even in the trees surrounding the house.

I finally decided to call the police. A police supervisor came out to the house and spoke to the media, warning them about trespassing on my property. He returned to the house and stayed and talked with us for a while, reassuring us that he would come back if we needed him to, and he gave us some advice about how to handle the media. Before he left, he expressed his sympathy for the situation our family was in and told us to call anytime we needed him. He was very empathetic and helpful. His kindness was appreciated very much at the time.

After the media were ordered off our property, they began to congregate on the sidewalks and on the street outside, waiting for any sign of movement from our house. When Melissa finally made an attempt to leave to go home, she had to run to the car with young Emily, with cameras being shoved in their faces and reporters on their heels. The reporters surrounded the car, preventing her from leaving. She was forced to run back into the house.

After we all calmed down somewhat, we came up with a strategy that would allow them to leave safely without being harassed. They were eventually able to make their escape but not without the media hot on their tails. The media followed her all the way home and converged on her place, where my mother also lived. My mother was in the yard and had to run inside and hide with the children. She kept screaming, "Go away! Leave us alone!"

My brother Eldon came by my house that evening to be with me. As he made his way through the crowd of hungry vultures that circled, waiting to pick at their next victim for information, he was bombarded with questions and asked to comment. He became livid and started yelling at them: "Back the FUCK off, stay away from me, our family, my sister, and her home!" When he finally got to the door, I was afraid to open it because I thought he was another reporter. He had to assure me that it was he and that it was okay.

I sat with him that night, talking about what was going on, and what had happened, but it's still just a blur to me, even to this day. My mind was racing in so many directions, and I started to have trouble speaking and even breathing. My head and heart were pounding. At one point I grabbed my brother's hand and said, "Something's wrong with me, I need to go to the hospital." He told me, "No, you can't go out there, they're everywhere. They'll swarm you and follow you to the hospital." He held onto me and kept repeating, "Calm down. Breathe. I'm here. You're going to be okay." As much as he tried to calm me, I could see the panic in his eyes, and I could feel his own heart pounding. The rest of that night is a blank. The last thing I remember is being in my brother's arms and hearing Conrad say, "I'm here, Mama, I won't leave you." He assured me he'd secured the house. My next recollection is being in my kitchen the following morning.

The media circus continued over the following days: letters, notes, cards, and gift baskets were dropped off and sent to our home from far and wide. Messages came sympathizing with our situation, requests for interviews and television appearances, offers to write books — anything to get us to talk. Some relentless reporters, despite being cautioned by the police not to trespass, came back onto our property, though less aggressively this time, with cameras still in hand, but not rolling, in a last-ditch effort to get an exclusive story. Our entire family remained tight-lipped and vigilant. We weren't talking. As a family, we collectively agreed not to talk publicly, and for good reason. Luka had still not been apprehended, and we knew there would be further police questioning and a trial down the road. We didn't want to impede this process in any way by something we might say. We also took into consideration that Luka might be watching the media coverage. What if seeing us talking about him publicly caused the crisis he was in to worsen?

The gravity of the situation was overwhelming for me. New articles were manifesting daily in the papers and on the television, full of details, rumors, and speculation about Luka and the crime. Through it all, we sat in hiding, trying to absorb each new bit of information. We clung to each other for support. It felt like we were all in the same sinking boat. How could we help each other when we were all in the same predicament? We decided we were going to stick together no matter what. Our family ties had been tested many times before. We had pulled through the sudden death of my younger sister, Andrea, in January 2010, and a house fire in my home in June of the same year. We'd supported each other through break-ups, divorces, custody battles, criminal charges, domestic violence, car accidents, injuries, illnesses, and deaths, but nothing could have prepared us for what we were now facing. So, with our previous battle wounds still healing, we donned our armor yet again and formulated a survival plan. We were going to have to rely heavily on each other's strengths. We sought love, faith, comfort, understanding, trust, encouragement, patience, wisdom, knowledge, and judgment from one another like never before, and together we kept our sinking lifeboat afloat.

http://wbp.bz/mstka

**AVAILABLE FROM ANNE K. HOWARD
AND WILDBLUE PRESS!**

HIS GARDEN by ANNE K. HOWARD

http://wbp.bz/hisgardena

Read A Sample Next

1.

July 25, 2003

The monster stirred inside him. Most times, he could tame it. Keep it hidden. Silence its screams. But tonight, the beast demanded release.

She lifted her head up. "You're taking too long. I'm done."

He pressed her head back down. "You're done when I say you're done ..."

She wriggled beneath the firmness of his grip. "No!" she protested, forcing herself up from his lap. She stared him straight in the eyes—defiant and unafraid. "That's all I'm doing for you, Devin."

His calloused fingertips nervously tapped the upholstered backbench and his spine tingled with an odd mixture of excitement and fear. The beast was rising. There was no going back. Not now. Not ever. "Rape her," the monster instructed. "Rape the whore!"

*

It had been a long night of hustling for Nilsa Arizmendi and Angel "Ace" Sanchez. Maybe it was the hot weather, but the regular johns were being especially cheap and irritable, and Nilsa was forced to negotiate smaller fees. Ordinarily, she charged $30 for a half hour, but tonight's tricks were turning a maximum of only $20 and some demanded blowjobs for a measly 10 bucks. Like shrewd customers at a turn-of-the-century street market, the johns knew that the vendor in question was desperate for cash.

Ace loitered around the corners of New Britain Avenue, where his girlfriend worked. He stared glumly at the filthy surroundings, trying not to think about Nilsa's activities. He did not like their lifestyle. In fact, he despised it. But how else could he and Nilsa score drugs? The couple's shared habit was not cheap. In July 2003, they were each smoking about 20 to 30 pieces of crack per day and shooting up a bundle-and-a-half of heroin, which translated to about 10 to 15 bags on the streets. Sometimes, Nilsa used up to three bundles of heroin a day, depending on the amount of crack she smoked. It was a nasty cycle. The crack got Nilsa and

Ace ramped up and wired and the heroin brought them down. They needed both to survive.

Without the drugs, sickness set in. Being drug sick was terrible—worse than having the flu. In the darkness of their motel room, the childhood sweethearts huddled together in sweat-soaked sheets, shivering with nausea and chills. Every joint and bone ached as invisible bugs furiously crawled beneath the surface of their skin. In between fits of vomiting, their bowels loosened and the bed became soiled. Nilsa kept the curtains drawn and placed the Do Not Disturb sign on the outside door handle for days at a time. The room was a mess. Their lives were a mess. Besides the incessant and all-consuming craving for heroin, she felt shame.

"This shit has to stop," Ace thought as he watched Nilsa emerge from the back seat of an old man's car. She walked toward him, tucked her tie-dyed T-shirt into her dungaree shorts and offered a faint smile. Normally 140 pounds, the 5'2", dark-haired woman was now only skin and bones. "I'm tired," she said. "Let's go home."

On the walk back, Nilsa briefly disappeared and scored a blast of crack at Goodwin Park in Hartford. She returned to Ace and attempted to take his hand. He pulled away. "I'm done with this shit. You gotta go to rehab, Nilsa. We both gotta go."

She acted like she did not hear him. It was usually the best way to avoid a fight.

But tonight, Ace would not let up. "I'm done with the fucking drugs," he mumbled, running his hand through his greasy dark hair. Normally, he kept it long, but a few days before, he had cut it short. "Done with the hustling. Fuck. Fuck this shit."

Their shadowy figures forged into the night, softly illuminated by the neon lights of outdated motels. Rolling hills of forest stood far in the distance, strangely comforting and yet somehow sinister. When Nilsa's high wore down, they started to quarrel. This time, Ace would not take no for an answer. They both had to go to rehab in the morning. Nilsa was reluctant. She had been in and out of rehab for years and it never did her any good. Still, she loved her four children and desperately wanted to be done with the drugs and get clean forever and for good. Overhead, the night sky opened and a warm drizzle began to fall. The blue rock watch on Nilsa's frail wrist ticked into the early morning hours. They walked southbound along the pike, past Cedar Hill Cemetery containing the corpses of Connecticut's affluent class, including legendary actress Katharine Hepburn, and then a smaller cemetery containing the remains of lesser-known citizens.

Ace gently elbowed Nilsa. "You gonna start singing?"

She sometimes sang Christian hymns that she learned in childhood as they walked along the pike. It passed the time and gave them both a sense of comfort in the midst of all the pain. She smiled beneath the foggy moonlight. "You want me to?"

"You know I like your voice," he replied.

Her smooth, clear voice chimed like a bell into the darkness of the night:

O Lord my God, When I in awesome wonder,

Consider all the worlds Thy Hands have made;

I see the stars, I hear the rolling thunder,

Thy power throughout the universe displayed.

By the time they reached the parking lot of the Stop & Shop in Wethersfield, Ace had persuaded Nilsa to agree to the plan. Nilsa was worthy of a long and healthy life. After all, Ace needed her. Her mother needed her. *Her children needed her.* She vowed to never turn another trick again or inject poison into her veins. The party was over and fuck her if it had not been the party from Hell.

Nilsa eyed a lone vehicle parked in the far corner of the store's lot. "That's Devin's van."

"Let's get back to the motel," Ace said.

"I'm just gonna say hi."

Nilsa walked across the lot to the beat-up blue van owned by their mutual acquaintance, Devin Howell. They had met Howell a few months before. At the time, he was pumping gas at the Exxon gas station on the corner of Broad Street and New Britain Avenue. The rain was heavy and Ace and Nilsa were soaking wet as they approached Howell's van and asked for a ride to their motel room on the Berlin Turnpike in Wethersfield. "We'll give you five bucks," Ace said.

Howell had to go to Lowe's to price out some supplies for an upcoming job. He was driving in that direction anyway, so it was not a problem to assist two near-strangers who appeared down on their luck. "Yeah, sure. The door's unlocked."

Nilsa and Ace squeezed into the bucket seat on the passenger side. Nilsa used her street name, Maria, when she introduced herself to Howell. As they drove to The Almar Motel, Howell told the couple in his mild Southern drawl that he had a lawn-care business. Ace glanced over his shoulder at the back of the van. The space was large, with a long bench sofa littered with lawn service tools and clothing. The stench of body odor pervaded the vehicle's interior.

When they arrived at the motel, Ace and Nilsa invited Howell into their room to hang out. Howell brought some beer and marijuana. Nilsa and Ace offered to share a little crack, but Howell refused. He was a weed and booze guy. Together, the three got high on their poisons of choice.

Howell told them that he was living in his van and he often parked it at the Stop & Shop parking lot in Wethersfield. He left the motel less than an hour later. As he drove back to the Stop & Shop lot to bed down for the night, he glanced at the open ashtray and saw that a $20 bill rolled up inside of it was gone. "No fucking good deed goes unpunished," he cynically thought. Ace and Nilsa had ripped him off.

In the months that followed, the occasional contact with Howell proved beneficial to Nilsa and Ace. The couple had lived on the Berlin Turnpike for the last 18 months or so, first at The Elm Motel and then at The Almar. Their daily routine involved walking from the motel on the pike to the familiar section of New Britain Avenue in Hartford where Nilsa turned tricks, about 1½ miles from The Almar. Ace had not worked a job for seven or eight months and he no longer had a vehicle of his own. Especially in the cold weather, Nilsa and Ace relied on acquaintances to spot them walking along the busy roadway and offer a lift. Occasionally, they had money for a cab, but that meant less money for drugs.

Howell also proved useful in assisting Nilsa and Ace to cop drugs. He did not mind driving them to local dealers living 15 to 20 minutes away. He would not get high with them when they scored. He seemed content to do them a favor by giving them a ride in exchange for a few dollars. All told, Howell served as the couple's makeshift Uber driver on about five occasions over the course of one month.

At approximately 2:45 a.m. on July 25, 2003, Ace watched Nilsa's skeletal form traipse across the empty parking lot. It was hard for him to believe that this was the same woman whose weight had sky-rocketed to 180 pounds when she was last released from federal prison—all beefed up by the cheap, starchy food. Nilsa stopped at the van and appeared to talk to Howell, who sat in the driver's seat. Then she walked around the van and got into the passenger side.

Howell turned on the engine and slowly drove away. It was the last time Ace would see Nilsa alive.

*

When Christ shall come, with shout of acclamation,

And take me home, what joy shall fill my heart.

Then I shall bow, in humble adoration,

And then proclaim: "My God, how great Thou art!"

Nilsa "Coco" Arizmendi, Jan. 29, 1970–July 25, 2003

Rest In Peace

2.

It's a strange thing, writing letters to an alleged serial killer. Stranger still is reading the letters that he writes back.

When I first contacted William Devin Howell in July 2015, he was serving a 15-year sentence for the murder of Nilsa Arizmendi. Howell had yet to be charged with the murders of six other victims whose bones were found in the same wooded area behind the strip mall in New Britain. Nonetheless, the tone of his first letter to me indicated that he knew that the remaining charges were about to slam down upon him with the force of a sledgehammer.

Two months earlier, Howell's image had been smeared across local and national news channels when Chief State's Attorney Kevin Kane named him as the main suspect in the New Britain serial killings. Kane's announcement was a long time coming. Howell told me that two years earlier, he refused to speak with police officers about the accusations without a lawyer present. His refusal to speak resulted in Howell being stripped of his industry job in prison as a kind of punishment by the Department of Corrections (D.O.C.). While not a big deal to a prison outsider, for an inmate who lives for a few extra dollars a week to purchase better quality soap or tinned spicy tuna at the prison commissary, it was a grave loss for Howell. He took pride in having an industry job. It paid a whopping $1 an hour compared to typical prison jobs that pay 75 cents a day. Howell explained to me that he had worked all his life, whether in lawn care or a pizza parlor or a 7-Eleven in Florida. No job was beneath him and it discouraged him to be sitting in isolation doing nothing.

In April 2015, after speaking with one of Howell's former cellmates, Jonathan Mills, who told investigators that Howell confessed many details of the crimes to him, police obtained a search warrant for Howell's cell at Garner Correctional Institution in Newtown, Conn., where he was being held at the time. The search warrant detailed items taken from the inmate's cell: a newspaper article about the death penalty in Florida; a notebook with handwritten entries that referenced darkvomit.com, a website that sold memorabilia associated with serial killers and other notorious murderers; and a cell phone bill from July 2003 with words written by Howell, "This just shows the day after I killed."

The newspaper article about the death penalty in Florida prompted authorities to look into whether Howell was behind the unsolved murder of April Marie Stone, 21, who went missing on Jan. 14, 1991, after she was seen walking along a state highway in South Apopka, Fla. Her body was found two days later beside a dirt road in nearby Sanford. She had been stabbed to death and wrapped in a blanket. At the time of the killing, Howell was living about 15 miles away in a trailer in Casselberry with his girlfriend, Mandy, and their infant son. A few months after police found Stone, Howell was charged with soliciting prostitution in Altamonte Springs, the next town over from Casselberry. He had approached the undercover officer in a blue Ford pickup truck and offered her $15 for oral sex, according to the arrest report. He entered a plea of guilty and avoided jail time by paying a fine. It was not until 2015, after Howell was charged with murdering six more victims found behind the strip mall in New Britain, that law enforcement looked into the possibility that he may have been behind Stone's murder in Florida, years before. Investigators in Florida looked into the matter, but did not find any evidence linking Howell to Stone's murder.

I never thought that Howell was behind the slaying of April Stone. She was not part of what appeared to be his target group—prostitutes, many with substance abuse issues—and her body, though wrapped in a blanket, was not buried. Additionally, although Howell had been accused of grisly atrocities—including slicing the fingertips of one of his victims and dismantling her jaw, death by stabbing did not conform to his apparent modus operandi.

I took a deep breath before writing my first letter to Howell, fully aware that I was about to step aboard Ozzy's proverbial Crazy Train with no hope of escape in the years ahead. Here is my letter of introduction:

July 19, 2015

RE: Correspondence and Visitation

Dear Mr. Howell:

I am doing some research and writing about the unsolved murders in New Britain. Since you are the main suspect, I would very much like to correspond with you and meet with you to discuss the allegations. Juliana Holcomb, the daughter of your ex-girlfriend Dorothy, describes you as a "kind-hearted giant." In personal photos, you appear to be a friendly individual who would not harm a fly. I would like to hear your side of the story in this matter.

Please write to me and let me know if I can get on your visitation list. I am a practicing attorney. However, I have no desire to become involved in any of the legal aspects of your incarceration. In my capacity as a journalist, I simply want to hear your side of the story.

Sincerely:

Anne K. Howard

Attorney at Law

And so began my relationship with a man that I believed would one day take the title of Connecticut's most prolific serial killer.

See even more at:
http://wbp.bz/tc

More True Crime You'll Love From WildBlue Press

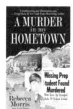

A MURDER IN MY HOMETOWN by Rebecca Morris

Nearly 50 years after the murder of seventeen year old Dick Kitchel, Rebecca Morris returned to her hometown to write about how the murder changed a town, a school, and the lives of his friends.

wbp.bz/hometowna

THE BEAST I LOVED by Robert Davidson

Robert Davidson again demonstrates that he is a master of psychological horror in this riveting and hypnotic story ... I was so enthralled that I finished the book in a single sitting. "—James Byron Huggins, International Bestselling Author of The Reckoning

wbp.bz/tbila

BULLIED TO DEATH by Judith A. Yates

On September 5, 2015, in a public park in LaVergne, Tennessee, fourteen-year-old Sherokee Harriman drove a kitchen knife into her stomach as other teens watched in horror. Despite attempts to save her, the girl died, and the coroner ruled it a "suicide." But was it? Or was it a crime perpetuated by other teens who had bullied her?

wbp.bz/btda

SUMMARY EXECUTION by Michael Withey

"An incredible true story that reads like an international crime thriller peopled with assassins, political activists, shady FBI informants, murdered witnesses, a tenacious attorney, and a murderous foreign dictator."—Steve Jackson, New York Times bestselling author of NO STONE UNTURNED

wbp.bz/sea

12316913R00144

Made in the USA
Monee, IL
24 September 2019